QUEEN OF SCOTS

ROSALIND K. MARSHALL

SCOTTISH NATIONAL PORTRAIT GALLERY
HISTORIC BUILDINGS AND MONUMENTS (SDD)
NATIONAL LIBRARY OF SCOTLAND
ROYAL MUSEUM OF SCOTLAND

BERNAN-UNIPUB

LANHAM MARYLAND 20706

Designed by HMSO Graphic Design. J Cairns

ISBN 0 527 35980 7

CONTENTS

ACKNOWLEDGMENTS

I am grateful to the owners of all the items included as illustrations in this book, in particular to Historic Buildings and Monuments, (SDD), and the Trustees of the National Galleries of Scotland, the National Library of Scotland and the National Museums of Scotland. The generous assistance of these institutions and the help of their curatorial and photographic staff is much appreciated. Individual acknowledgments are to be found in the captions. I would also thank Professor Gordon Donaldson, HM Historiographer in Scotland for reading the completed text and Dr David Breeze, Professor Sir Jack Dewhurst, Dr David Caldwell, Miss Fiona Stewart, Mrs Dana Mayer and Mr Alastair Cherry for their kind advice on a variety of points.

R.K.M.
Edinburgh, July 1986

NOTE ON SOURCES

All the direct speech which I have quoted is taken from the various recollections of those people who were present at the time. Some of the sources are in Scots, some are in English and some are in French. I have translated the French and several of the more obscure Scottish words into English, and I have modernised spelling and punctuation.

1. *James V and Mary of Guise*, parents of Mary, Queen of Scots, by an unknown artist. (The Duke of Atholl, at Blair Castle)

1

A SAD INHERITANCE

IN THE early days of December 1542, King James V of Scotland lay dying in his palace of Falkland. He was a young man still, only thirty years old, but his armies had been routed, his policies lay in ruins and his two infant sons were dead. He could endure no more.

'Where will Your Grace spend Christmas?' his servants asked anxiously, seeking to rouse him from his despair, but he only smiled grimly and replied,

'I cannot tell. Choose ye the place. But this I can tell you. On Yule Day you will be masterless and the realm without a king.'

In vain did his doctors ply him with their herbal potions. He lay uncaring, knowing no one, murmuring over and over to himself,

'All is lost, all is lost.'

His courtiers could only pray that news would come from Linlithgow, good news, to revive his courage, for his queen was there, awaiting the birth of another child.

2. The lion rampant of Scotland, carved on the gateway of Linlithgow Palace. (Historic Buildings and Monuments, SDD)

At last a rider came into view, spurring his horse on till he reached the palace gates, but the message he brought was not the one they wanted to hear. The Queen, he said, was safely delivered, but there was no son and heir. The baby was a girl. They had to tell the King, of course, for there was no avoiding it, and perhaps even the thought of a daughter would catch his attention. He listened to them silently, remembered how the crown had come to his ancestors through the daughter of Robert the Bruce, and in that moment he knew that all hope was truly gone. In his troubled country no girl could possibly keep the throne.

'It cam' wi' a lass and it will gang wi' a lass,' he said, and he turned his face to the wall.

It was 8 December. He lingered on for a few days more, slipping in and out of consciousness, raving in delirium. At about midnight on the 14th, he suddenly opened his eyes and looked at the little group of courtiers who were keeping watch by his bed. He seemed to recognise them for the first time in days, for he gave a little smile, laughed weakly, kissed his hand to them, and then he died. His daughter Mary, at six days old, became Queen of Scots.

3. The fleur-de-lys of France, carved on the gateway of Linlithgow Palace. (Historic Buildings and Monuments, SDD)

The news of the King's death shocked the nation. At first, people could hardly believe it. His illness had certainly been well-known, but no one had looked for a fatal outcome and the country was thrown into confusion. The victorious English army was poised for a new invasion, to follow up its resounding success at Solway Moss, the realm was left leaderless and there were doubts about the survival of the baby at Linlithgow. Amidst all the uncertainty, rumour was rife and it was widely reported that the King's daughter was so weak that she would not survive, and even that she was already dead.

As the days went by, however, the immediate crisis passed and there

4. *Solway Moss*, scene of the battle of 1542, painted in the nineteenth century by William Simson. (National Gallery of Scotland)

5. The ruins of Holyrood Abbey, where Mary's father was buried. (Reproduced by gracious permission of Her Majesty The Queen: photograph, A. Forbes)

6. *Henry VIII of England*, uncle and enemy of Mary's father, by an unknown artist. (National Portrait Gallery, London)

was a strange, calm interlude. The threat of invasion was temporarily removed when the English general told Henry VIII that it 'should not be to Your Majesty's honour that we, your soldiers, should make war or invade upon a dead body or upon a widow or on a young suckling, his daughter, and specially upon the time of the funerals of the said King, at which time all his realm must lament the same'. Accordingly, he observed a truce, but the Scots knew that they had been granted no more than a brief respite.

Meanwhile, it was also becoming clear that the infant Queen would survive, and her companions at Linlithgow devoted themselves to her care. The palace there stands on the banks of a small loch, its handsome stone walls rising high above a central courtyard with an elaborately carved fountain. Much of the building is ruined now, but in 1542 it was an elegant place, a favourite residence of the royal family, who visited it at least once each year. Then the great presence chambers were hung with tapestries. Sumptuous velvet and lace beds were erected in the private rooms and a veritable army of cooks toiled over the spits and cauldrons in the kitchens. Everywhere there were servants clad in livery: scarlet and yellow for members of the royal household, black for the French retinue of James V's wife. In times of rejoicing, the fountain in the courtyard ran with wine.

There were no such celebrations when Mary, Queen of Scots was born, nor have we any description of her christening. It presumably took place some time in December in the church of St Michael, which stands just beside the palace gate. All we know is that the Lord Treasurer authorised payment of fifty-four shillings for white taffeta 'to the Princess's baptism'.

7. Linlithgow Palace, from the loch.
(Historic Buildings and Monuments, SDD)

Neither his clerks nor anyone else had yet come to terms with the fact that the baby in the palace was no mere Princess but a monarch in her own right.

Tightly wrapped in her swaddling clothes, in keeping with the custom of the time, Mary, Queen of Scots spent the first weeks of her life lying in her cradle in her mother's apartments at the north-west corner of the palace. The windows looked directly out over the dark waters of the loch and a huge fire blazed in the great stone hearth. It was an exceptionally cold winter.

The infant may have been premature, as some people said, but she was a fine, healthy child. She soon gained weight and she was obviously thriving under the careful attentions of her mother and her Scottish wet-nurse. Indeed, she had her own retinue of attendants ready to anticipate her every need: nurses to change her swaddling bands, bathe her and wash her linen. There were even special women to rock her cradle. When Sir Ralph Sadler, an English envoy, came to call on the Queen Mother, Mary of Guise, in March, he made the mistake of referring

8. Inside the north-west tower of Linlithgow Palace, with the second floor room where Mary was born. (Historic Buildings and Monuments, SDD)

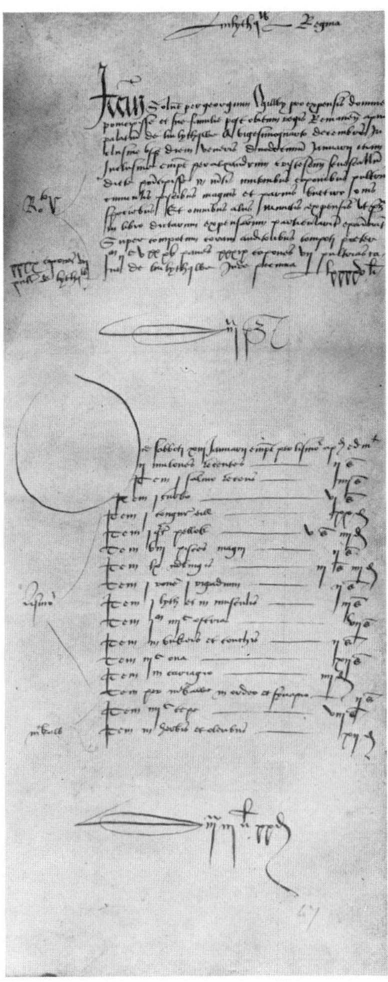

9. The expenses of the Royal Household at Linlithgow in the winter of 1542–3, showing sums spent on salmon, turbot and '1 congur eill'. (Scottish Record Office)

10. The Great Hall of Linlithgow Palace. (Historic Buildings and Monuments, SDD)

11. The Chapel at Linlithgow Palace. (Historic Buildings and Monuments, SDD)

to reports that the baby was delicate. Mary of Guise indignantly retorted that these were lies, put about by one of her enemies.

'You shall see whether he says true or not!' she exclaimed, and she ordered one of the nurses to bring the child. She then had her daughter unwrapped from her swaddling bands and Sir Ralph was forced to admit that 'it is as goodly a child as I have seen, of her age'. Satisfied, Mary of Guise drew his attention to the baby's size, remarking with a sidelong smile that one day the baby would be as tall as she was herself and she, said Sir Ralph somewhat ruefully, was 'of the largest size of women'.

He was wary of the Queen Mother because she was French, a daughter of the house of Guise, the proud and ancient family which claimed descent from the Emperor Charlemagne himself. She was no foolish young girl, either. She had come to Scotland as a widow, and she had soon proved to be an astute and ambitious consort for James V. Indeed, it would have been better for him had he paid more attention to her advice. However, it was too late for that now, and it was obvious that she was directing all her formidable energies into the protection of his one surviving legitimate child.

Sir Ralph wrote a detailed account of the encounter, for his master, Henry VIII, was deeply interested in everything that was happening in Scotland. For centuries, the Scots and the French had been the traditional enemies of England and Henry had long since resolved that he must destroy the friendship between them. It was far too dangerous for it meant that his country was liable to be attacked from both the north and the south. James V was his nephew, but there had been no friendship

12. *James Hamilton, Earl of Arran*, head of the Hamilton family and Regent of Scotland during Mary's early childhood, by an unknown artist. (The Duke of Hamilton, at Lennoxlove)

13. Inside Kinneil House, one of the homes of the Regent Arran. (Historic Buildings and Monuments, SDD)

between them. Henry claimed to be overlord of Scotland, then he had defeated James's army but as soon as he heard that his nephew was dead he saw that he could get what he wanted without having recourse to another expensive military campaign. The King of Scots had left a daughter. He himself had a young son. If the two were to marry, he could rule over Scotland on behalf of his daughter-in-law and his foreign problems would be at an end.

To the modern mind, the idea of a child marriage is bizarre, but in the sixteenth century it was an accepted fact of life that if two Kings wished to make an alliance or two powerful families wanted to strengthen their friendship, the best way to proceed was to arrange a wedding between children of both families. The happiness of the individuals involved was never really considered. What mattered was that lands or wealth would be united and in theory, at least, there would be an indissoluble bond between the new relations.

Henry was optimistic. No one was going to object to his scheme on the grounds that Mary was only a few weeks old, Price Edward just five, and there were plenty of Protestants in Scotland who would welcome a closer relationship with England. The sooner he acted, the better it would be, for the Scots were still in a state of chaos. The Queen Mother had failed to become Regent and instead James, Earl of Arran was ruling as Lord Governor. He was head of the powerful house of Hamilton and next heir to the throne should anything happen to the infant Queen, but he was a weak and irresolute man who was readily manipulated. A little judicious bribery and some alluring promises never to be kept worked wonders. By

14. *Edward VI of England,* son of Henry VIII, betrothed to Mary, by an unknown artist. (Reproduced by gracious permission of Her Majesty The Queen)

the time spring came, Henry had his way. When the Scottish parliament met in March, the delegates agreed to appoint commissioners to discuss a possible marriage agreement. On 1 July, negotiations were complete and the Treaties of Greenwich were drawn up.

The first treaty said that there would be peace between Scotland and England throughout the lifetimes of Henry VIII and Mary, Queen of Scots. The second treaty announced that 'the illustrious and noble Prince Edward, eldest son and nearest apparent and undoubted heir of the unconquered and most potent Prince, Henry VIII' should take as his wife 'Mary, Queen of Scotland, now also a minor and not yet out of her first year'. Because of her age, the wedding could not take place yet, but as soon as she reached her eleventh birthday she would be married by proxy, travel to England, and stay at Court. In the meantime, Henry would send north some English nobleman and his wife, with their attendants, and they would live in the infant Queen's household, have access to her at all times and oversee both her feeding and her education. Scotland would, of course, remain an independent kingdom both before and after the wedding.

That safeguard was all very well, but would Henry keep his word? The Scots were sure that he would not. As soon as the terms of the treaties were made public, there was an outcry. Many people feared that Henry would never have the patience to wait ten years. They were convinced that he would demand, or even seize, the Queen at the earliest possible moment. In the past, he had plotted to kidnap James V. Now, with an English family staying in the royal household, it would be all too easy for him to concoct a similar scheme and if that happened the Scots would lose not only their monarch but their independence.

Popular feeling ran high. Sir Ralph Sadler's archery targets in his Edinburgh garden were despoiled and as he walked behind his lodgings with some friends a shot was fired, narrowly missing them. No one could speak of anything but the infamous treaties and, terrified in case the English should sail up the Firth of Forth, Mary of Guise decided that her daughter must be moved to a place of greater safety than Linlithgow.

Further up the Forth stood the castle of Stirling, perched on a high rock above the valley. It would be far easier to resist an attack there, the Queen Mother knew, and so she persuaded the Regent to allow her to take Mary there. For days, horses went to and fro across the Lowlands of Scotland carrying all the equipment necessary for the royal household. Twenty-four carriage horses bore Mary of Guise's great bed and the beds of her ladies in waiting. One man, specially chosen, was entrusted with carrying the little Queen's cradle, while another looked after the royal pictures. Nineteen carriage horses transported the contents of the great larder, all the kitchen utensils and the equipment of wine cellar and bakehouse. Finally, when the furnishings had gone, the royal party set out. Escorted by an army of two and a half thousand mounted soldiers and a thousand heavily armed footsoldiers, Mary, Queen of Scots made her first journey across her kingdom.

Events moved swiftly after that. Impatient and irascible, Henry VIII demanded that the Scots should break off their old alliance with France at once, and he made it plain that he certainly would not wait ten years to take charge of his son's future bride. Mary, Queen of Scots was to come to London as soon as she was old enough to leave her mother. So confident was he that he did not even bother to ratify the Treaties of Greenwich within two months' time as he ought to have done, and when he ordered the seizure of some of their ships on the high seas, the Scots realised that they had made a terrible mistake. The marriage agreement could not be allowed to go ahead.

On 9 September 1543, Mary, Queen of Scots, now nine months old, was crowned in the Chapel Royal at Stirling, as a sign to the whole world that Scotland was an independent nation with its own rightful monarch. In December, parliament denounced the Treaties of Greenwich and declared them to be totally null and void. Henry VIII was furious. The impudent Scots could not be allowed to defy him in this way. They had agreed to the marriage and they must abide by the Treaties whether they liked them or not. As soon as the better weather came the following spring

15. *Edward, Earl of Hertford and later Duke of Somerset,* commander of the English army, by an unknown artist. (Reproduced by permission of the Marquess of Bath, Longleat House, Wiltshire: photograph, the Courtauld Institute of Art, London)

he launched a full-scale invasion of Scotland. 'Put all to fire and the sword,' he told his commander, the Earl of Hertford. 'Burn Edinburgh town, so razed and defaced when you have sacked and gotten what you can of it, as there may remain forever a perpetual memory of the vengeance of God lightened upon the Scots for their falsehood and disobedience.'

During the next four years, Scotland suffered a series of devastating attacks from the south. That first summer the English entered Edinburgh, setting fire to the Abbey of Holyroodhouse where James V lay buried, as well as destroying many houses in the town and along the coast. The following year they came in harvest time and burned the crops in the fertile Tweed valley, setting ablaze the abbeys of Melrose, Jedburgh and Dryburgh as they went.

While his forces were busy in the north, Henry VIII was plotting the elimination of one of his most powerful enemies in Scotland. Cardinal David Beaton was the leading Catholic prelate there and a staunch friend of France. Various schemes aimed at assassinating him were drawn up with Henry's approval, for there was no lack of people who hated the able, wily Cardinal. Protestant opinions were gaining ground throughout Scotland and for those of the Reformed faith, Beaton represented everything that was corrupt and decadent about the old religion. Finally, in May 1546, the Cardinal was stabbed to death in his own castle of St Andrews by a group of men avenging the death of George Wishart, a Protestant preacher whom he had sent to the stake. The murderers hung their victim's body by the left arm and the left leg from the very window at which he had sat and watched Wishart burn, then they held the castle on behalf of the English for many months.

Against this background of fear and violence, Mary, Queen of Scots was growing into a bright, lively child. Safe in her castle, she had not only the

16. *Cardinal David Beaton*, Scotland's leading churchman, by an unknown artist from an earlier portrait. (The Trustees of Blairs College, Aberdeen: photograph, *Scotland's Story*)

17. St Andrews Castle, Fife, where Cardinal Beaton was murdered. (Historic Buildings and Monuments, SDD)

18. Underground passage dug at St Andrews Castle during the siege which followed Beaton's murder. (Historic Buildings and Monuments, SDD)

MARY'S SCOTTISH RELATIVES

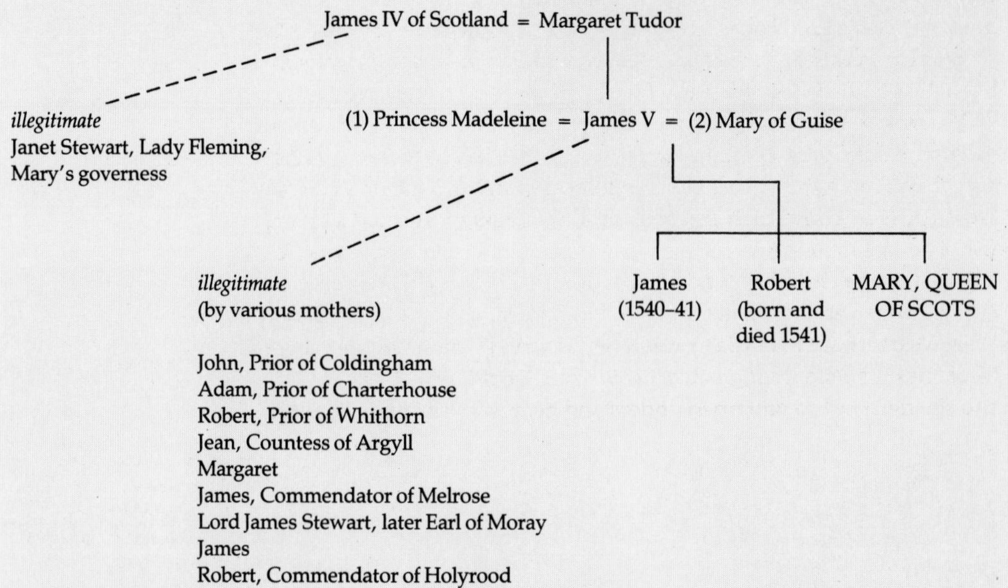

John, Prior of Coldingham
Adam, Prior of Charterhouse
Robert, Prior of Whithorn
Jean, Countess of Argyll
Margaret
James, Commendator of Melrose
Lord James Stewart, later Earl of Moray
James
Robert, Commendator of Holyrood

attentions of the anxious Queen Mother and her household, but she had young companions too: the children of the courtiers and her own half-brothers and sisters. In the sixteenth century, the illegitimate offspring of a great man were accepted members of his household, and James V had fathered a large brood of children outside wedlock. A highly-strung, neurotic young man, he had nevertheless been attractive to women with his thick red hair, his red-brown eyes and his narrow, foxy features. By the time he was twenty he had three illegitimate sons and he had at least six other natural children after that. They were all older than Mary, but when Lord James, Lord Robert and the others were not away at school she spent time in their company, and her mother was bringing up her half-sister Lady Jean Stewart almost as if she were her own child.

Of course, it was Mary who was the centre of attention and everyone delighted in her progress. She was, as she always had been, large for her age, with dark auburn hair like her mother's and her father's narrow brown eyes set above high cheekbones. Full of energy, she had a strong will of her own and she was obviously quick and intelligent. Moreover, for all her own French background and her devotion to her native land, Mary of Guise was very conscious that her daughter's future lay in Scotland. Whatever marriage might be made for her, wherever she might live in later life, James V's child was Queen of Scots. God had set her in that position, and she must be brought up to understand her responsibilities. The little

19. *Sir James Wilsford,* English commander, who held Haddington after its capture from the Scots: in the background is a view of the town. Portrait by an unknown artist. (Scottish National Portrait Gallery)

20. Penny of Mary, Queen of Scots, 1553. (National Museums of Scotland)

girl learned to speak in Scots, and although she was surrounded by her mother's French household neither Mary of Guise nor anyone else ever taught her French, so that until she was almost six, Scots was the only language she spoke.

For many months the little Queen's future looked grim indeed. Henry VIII died in January 1547, but that brought no relief since it was the Earl of Hertford who now ruled England on behalf of the young Edward VI. That autumn Hertford, now Duke of Somerset, marched once more across the Border at the head of an army of sixteen thousand men and the defeat he inflicted on the Scots at Pinkie, near Musselburgh, was known ever after as 'Black Saturday'. Many of the nation's nobles died in the conflict and the Lord Chancellor, the Earl of Huntly, was among those who were taken prisoner. The country was in a state of panic as the Lords in typical manner wrangled and blamed each other for the disaster. They sent Mary, Queen of Scots to the secluded island of Inchmahome, on the Lake of Menteith, for greater safety and finally they faced the unpalatable truth. Unless they had outside help, nothing could save them from the English armies.

At that low point in Scotland's fortunes, the French came to the rescue, not from any particularly charitable motives but simply because it was not in their interests to let Scotland be taken over by the English. Already they had assisted with small detachments of soldiers, and it was their fleet which had finally recaptured St Andrews Castle from the murderers of Cardinal Beaton. All along, Mary of Guise and her friends had been anxious to maintain the old alliance with France, but many Scots found the French connection both distasteful and threatening. The soldiers who came from France seemed offensively foreign in their ways, and the Scots resented the fact that the French made no secret of their contempt for what they obviously regarded as a primitive, backward nation.

By the spring of 1548, though, when yet another English army was on its way north, the Scots finally decided that their only hope of salvation lay with France, and at this vital moment the French King, Henry II, sent over an exciting new proposition. For ten years he and his wife, Catherine de Medici, had been childless. During that time, Catherine consulted doctors, astrologers and even sorcerers in her attempts to have a baby. All her efforts were in vain until she started taking pills made from myrrh and

21. Inchmahome Priory, where Mary was sent for safety.
(Historic Buildings and Monuments, SDD)

22. *Mary of Guise*, attributed to Corneille de Lyon.
(Scottish National Portrait Gallery)

23. St Mary's Church, Haddington: the treaty was signed at the nearby nunnery. (Photograph, Michael Brooks)

then she suddenly discovered that she was pregnant. Her first son, Francis, was born in January 1544. An undersized, delicate infant, he had somehow managed to survive and now he was four. One day he would be King of France so what more suitable wife could be found for him than the Queen of Scots? By the marriage, France and Scotland would be united forever and England would be trapped irrevocably between them.

When they received Henry II's proposal, the Scots hesitated, stunned by the enormous implications. Mary of Guise was delighted, though, and the French King quickly followed up his suggestion with promises of military assistance. The situation was desperate and the Scots could not resist the thought of a powerful, active ally. They replied, accepting enthusiastically.

In June, the French fleet was sighted off Dunbar. It made an impressive spectacle, for there were over a hundred vessels, including sixteen galleys, a brigantine and three great ships. They landed their men at Leith and then they marched out to besiege Haddington, an important market town which had been occupied by the English. In the nunnery there, on 6 July 1548, the new treaty was signed. Never now to be the bride of Edward VI, Mary, Queen of Scots would instead marry the Dauphin Francis, heir to the French throne, 'to the perpetual honour, pleasure and profit of both realms'. Promising to respect Scotland's ancient liberty and laws, Henry II

24. Dumbarton Castle, where Mary stayed before she sailed for France. (Historic Buildings and Monuments, SDD)

said that he would defend that country as though it were his own.

There was every reason to suppose that the Treaty of Haddington would secure a glorious future for Mary, Queen of Scots, but it brought with it a painful decision for mother and daughter. The English were sure to be furious when they heard the details and there was no knowing what they might do in revenge. In all probability they would try to snatch the young Queen and marry her forcibly to Edward VI. Her life was in greater danger than ever and so, to save her from harm, it was suggested that she be sent to France at once, to her new family.

Ever a realist, Mary of Guise could see the sense of this proposal but it brought her much anguish. By her first husband, a French Duke, she had had two sons. One died in infancy and she had to leave the other behind in France when she married James V. She bore the Scottish King two more sons, but neither of them survived and so her emotional attachment to her daughter was particularly strong. The little Queen was the dear companion of her troubled hours in this turbulent foreign land. Her own Guise relatives urged her to leave the Scots to their own devices and travel back to France with the child but that she could never do. She was determined to protect her daughter's inheritance at all costs. She would remain in Scotland but, however much torment it cost her, she would send Mary, Queen of Scots to safety.

2

THE DAUPHIN'S BRIDE

SOME MONTHS earlier, the little Queen had been moved to Dumbarton Castle and the French galleys which had brought soldiers to Leith now sailed round the north coast of Scotland to the Clyde estuary. There, the Queen Mother, weeping, put her daughter on board. With the child went a large retinue led by her official guardians, Lord Erskine and Lord Livingston. Her nurse, Jean Sinclair, went along too and so did her governess, Lady Fleming, a fascinating widow who was herself a half-sister of James V. Three of Mary's half-brothers also accompanied her, although the eldest, Lord James, was to make only a brief stay at the French Court.

Apart from these boys, there was a crowd of children of Mary's own age, the sons and daughters of the nobility. The most celebrated members of this group were the small girls known as 'the four Maries'. A Queen always had maids-of-honour, and in Scotland they were termed 'Maries', from an old Icelandic word meaning a maiden. It was particularly appropriate that on this occasion they all had Mary as their first name: Mary Fleming, Mary Livingston, Mary Beaton and Mary Seton.

With so many young people on board there was a great deal of excitement, and they must have found it all the more frustrating when the commander of the fleet announced that there would be a delay before they could leave. Contrary winds were blowing and although the galleys were rowed by large numbers of men, they could not possibly depart in the teeth of a gale. For a whole week the vessels tossed on the Clyde until at last, on 7 August 1548, they set sail.

Unfortunately, as soon as they got out to the open sea, they encountered the most appalling weather. Fierce gales blew up again and raged without respite as the galleys battled their way down the west coast of England and round the shores of Wales. The worst moment came off Cornwall, when the rudder of the royal galley was smashed by heavy seas. There was an immediate panic among all the passengers except the Queen of Scots. She remained unperturbed, apparently enjoying the excitement as the sailors struggled to fit another rudder in place of the damaged one. Somehow or other, they managed it, and the frightening voyage continued.

At intervals, the commander of the galleys sent back detailed reports to Mary of Guise, telling her that her daughter was one of the few passengers to be unaffected by sea sickness. Perhaps he said this merely to reassure her, but it was probably true, for the Queen Mother was herself an excellent sailor. At any rate, when the battered galleys thankfully dropped anchor near the little village of Roscoff in Brittany, the child was perfectly fit and well. There, on 13 August, she set foot in France for the first time.

The countryside might be new to her but she, more than any of her companions, knew by name and reputation many of the people she would meet in the months ahead. Both her grandparents were still alive: Claud,

25. 'Mary Stuart Tower' at Roscoff, where Mary landed in France. (French Government Tourist Office)

26. 'Mary Stuart House', Roscoff. (French Government Tourist Office)

Duke of Guise, handsome and commanding, with an awe-inspiring military reputation, and his wife Antoinette, small, vivacious, devoted to the Catholic Church and to her family but with a quick sense of humour which made her an approachable and entertaining companion.

The Duchess had brought up Mary's half-brother, the little boy Mary of Guise had been forced to leave behind in France. Francis, Duke of Longueville, was nearly thirteen now, old enough to take part in Court ceremonial in his capacity as Grand Chamberlain of France, old enough, even, to ride with the French King's armies when they fought in Italy. Antoinette saw to it, though, that 'the little Duke', as they called him, never forgot his mother and now he was looking forward to making the acquaintance of the half-sister he had never seen.

Apart from Francis, Mary had many other French relatives, led by her six uncles and three aunts, important and influential men and women. Some of them had already played a vital part in their country's dealings with Scotland, and they all awaited the arrival of the Queen of Scots with an avid interest which owed as much to ambition as it did to natural affection.

Henry II was out of the country that August, campaigning yet again in Italy, and he had the little Duke with him. Mary, Queen of Scots was therefore able to make a leisurely progress through northern France to the castle of Carrières, near St Germain, where the French royal children were staying, and it was in this medieval fortress that she met her future husband for the first time.

The eagle-eyed French courtiers noted with satisfaction that the two children took to one another right away. Those who observed the painful contrast between them suppressed their doubts, but the difference in

MARY'S FRENCH RELATIVES

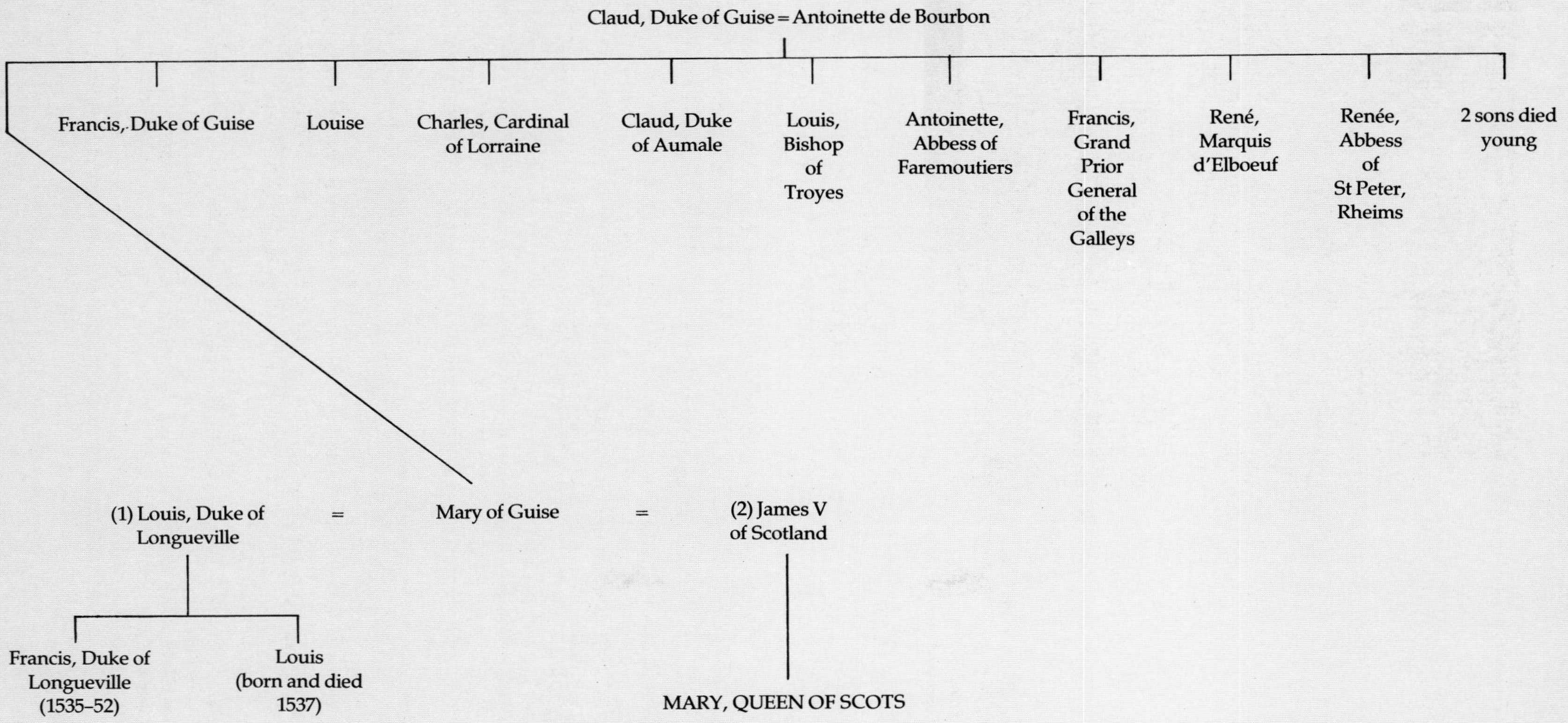

Claud, Duke of Guise = Antoinette de Bourbon

Francis, Duke of Guise
Louise
Charles, Cardinal of Lorraine
Claud, Duke of Aumale
Louis, Bishop of Troyes
Antoinette, Abbess of Faremoutiers
Francis, Grand Prior General of the Galleys
René, Marquis d'Elboeuf
Renée, Abbess of St Peter, Rheims
2 sons died young

(1) Louis, Duke of Longueville = Mary of Guise = (2) James V of Scotland

Children of (1) Louis, Duke of Longueville and Mary of Guise:
Francis, Duke of Longueville (1535–52)
Louis (born and died 1537)

Child of Mary of Guise and (2) James V of Scotland:
MARY, QUEEN OF SCOTS

27. *The Dauphin Francis*, aged about five, by an artist of the school of Clouet.
(Musée Condé, Chantilly: photograph, Giraudon)

28. *Henry II of France*, Mary's father-in-law, by François Clouet.
(The Bibliothèque Nationale, Paris)

29. *Catherine de Medici*, Mary's mother-in-law, by François Clouet.
(The Bibliothèque Nationale, Paris)

30. The Palace of Fontainbleau, where Mary often stayed with the French Court. (French Government Tourist Office)

31. *Claud, Duke of Guise,* Mary's grandfather, by an unknown artist. (The Bibliothèque Nationale, Paris)

32. *Princess Elisabeth of France,* Mary's childhood friend, by an unknown artist. (The Bibliothèque Nationale, Paris)

33. Chambord, another residence of the French Court.
(French Government Tourist Office)

physique was all too obvious. At almost six, the Queen of Scots was tall, sturdy and full of life. Four-year-old Francis was far smaller than he ought to be, with pale, puffy features and a heavy, lethargic body. His health had been poor from birth and spiteful courtiers blamed his condition on the unlikely pills and potions which his mother had swallowed during her frantic efforts to conceive a child. Both Henry II and Catherine de Medici doted on him, and they were in a constant state of anxiety about him, for it was obvious to everyone that it would be a miracle if this delicate, stunted child survived to inherit his father's throne.

Luckily, Mary seemed to see nothing amiss in her pallid and unprepossessing companion. Her warm heart was touched by his smallness and his timidity, and from the start she became his fiercely loving protector while he trotted along in her wake, happy to follow the lead of his high-spirited new playmate. The usually cynical French Lords looked on with a surprisingly sentimental approval. The Dauphin was as considerate and as loving as if Mary were already his wife, one of them

34. *The Dauphin Francis,* aged about seven, by an unknown artist. (Musée Condé, Chantilly: photograph, Giraudon)

remarked. 'It is very easy to see that God made them for each other,' he added, and that was the general opinion.

The Dauphin was not the only child in the royal nurseries, for after her slow start, Catherine de Medici was producing other children in quick succession. There were already two young princesses, Elisabeth who was two, and Claude, who was still a baby. Mary was put in the same bedchamber as Elisabeth and they grew up together like sisters, sharing a close affection.

It was pleasing, of course, that the children enjoyed each others' company, but what really mattered was the opinion of the King, and everyone waited in trepidation for Henry II's return. At long last, on 9 November, he appeared, and almost at once, happy and relieved reports flew back to Scotland. The King was delighted with Mary. From then onwards, the letters home to her mother were full of the praise lavished upon her for her intelligence, her grace and her good behaviour. Henry's initial opinion was confirmed as the months went by, and he treated her as though she were one of his own children.

He was disturbed, however, to discover that she spoke no French. He gave instructions that she was to start learning that language immediately and so that she would pick it up more rapidly he announced that in future all her servants should be French. Before anyone had time to protest, he sent the four Maries away to a convent at Poissy, where he said they would be properly educated. He also expressed the intention of removing Lady Fleming from her position as governess and appointing a French lady in her place.

If Mary was upset at losing her friends, her uncles were positively alarmed when they found out. Accustomed as they were to the intrigues of the Court, they realised at once that their niece's need to learn the language was merely an excuse for separating her from her retinue. Under Henry's care, she was to lose her own identity, becoming just another princess in his family circle, instead of a monarch in her own right. That would reduce their own importance as well as hers, and so it could not be allowed to happen. Mary of Guise took exactly the same view and she refused to allow Lady Fleming to be displaced. Eventually, Henry was even persuaded to announce that Mary was to take precedence over his own daughters, and so for the time being the Guise uncles were mollified.

Mary herself was still too young to understand all the undercurrents around her, and she was enjoying her new life. The Court never stayed for long in one place and so there were constantly new residences to explore, new people to meet. From Renaissance palace to imposing medieval fortress, they made their stately progress. Each building was more handsomely furnished than the one before, so it seemed, with fine tapestries, elegant furniture and beautiful paintings. For the adults, there was a constant round of feasting, dancing and playacting, and no doubt the royal children were allowed to watch some of the spectacles.

Certainly, the routine of their nursery was enlivened by visits from magnificently clad courtiers ready to fuss over and indulge the little Princes and Princesses. Almost each year a new baby joined the family: after Elisabeth and Claude there came Charles, Henry and Marguerite. From the day of her arrival, the Queen of Scots had established herself as the leader of the little group, not only because she was the eldest, but by reason of her strong personality and her decided opinions. Never tiring, always ready to think up some new diversion, she looked after the little ones with tender affection and whenever the Dauphin was ill or unhappy, he turned to her for comfort.

Two years after she left Scotland, she received a welcome visit from her mother. Mary of Guise came to France to persuade Henry II that he must send her yet more military assistance, for the Reformation was gaining ground in Scotland, and she stayed on for almost a year. On a personal level, she welcomed the opportunity for a reunion with both her daughter and the little Duke. She and eight-year-old Mary grew closer than ever, and the child heard long tales of all the difficulties in Scotland. When, on the eve of her mother's departure, the little Duke fell ill and died, they were united in their bitter grief.

Her mother's return to Scotland was unsettling for Mary, and other aspects of her life were changing too. In 1550 Lady Fleming was sent home in disgrace. Flamboyant and outspoken, she had caught the eye of the notoriously susceptible Henry II. They became lovers, much to the fury of both Catherine de Medici and Henry's principal mistress, Diane de Poitiers. When Lady Fleming was indiscreet enough to become pregnant, Catherine and Diane combined to oust her. A French lady, Madame de Parois, became Mary's governess instead. As temperamental in her own way as her predecessor had been, she was soon quarrelling with the

Ma Dame le Roy vous envoye Mons[r] de Breize qui m'a comme
scavez fait de bon coeur treshumble service, et de iour en autre s'efforce
de faire chose qui me soit agreable, qui me fait vous prier de bon coeur
luy faire bon recueil, et luy faire entendre que vous ay prie de ce
faire. Il a commandement du Roy vous conter amplement de
toutes nouvelles, qui me garde vous faire plus longue lettre si non
vous supplier treshumblement me entretenir tousiours en vostre
bonne grace comme,

Vostre treshumble et tresobeissante fille
Marie

35. Letter written by Mary to her mother, when she was about eight, recommending the French gentleman who was to deliver it.
(Scottish Record Office)

governesses of the Princesses, spending extravagantly and stirring up trouble among the entire household.

Despite these distractions, Mary was making good progress in her education. By the time she was twelve, she was beginning to learn Latin and she would also study Italian, Spanish and Greek. Her mother was most anxious, too, that her spiritual life should not be neglected and so she heard Mass every day. She had two chaplains of her own, one French and one Scottish. Nor were the social accomplishments neglected. Masters taught her to draw, dance and sing and she learned to play the lute. Listening to music and writing poetry were among her favourite diversions. She was also growing rapidly, and if Madame de Parois had any complaint about her it was that she stooped instead of holding herself

36. The earliest known picture of Mary, drawn when she was nine and a half, probably for Catherine de Medici, by an unknown artist.
(Musée Condé, Chantilly: photograph, Giraudon)

37. Scottish coin with Mary's profile, issued in 1557.
(National Museums of Scotland)

erect; not surprising, perhaps, when she was so much taller than her companions.

She was becoming increasingly aware of her own appearance, in fact, and in the autumn of 1554 when there was to be a lavish Court wedding she was much taken up with the outfit she would wear. At the last big occasion she had attended, she had been put out to discover that the Princesses were arrayed in gowns of cloth of gold and silver, while her own dress had merely been of silk. She announced that this time she must have a gold dress too, sewn all over with her royal cipher, in keeping with the latest fashion. She would complete this ensemble with a fine necklace of rubies and pearls, then she would be sure that nobody could outshine her.

An awareness of her own position in life lay behind her desire not to be outdone and she was starting to assert herself. She enjoyed giving orders, her governess reported. In case Mary of Guise took this as a sign that she was too headstrong, Madame de Parois hastened to add that when she did so she was, of course, merely passing on instructions from the Queen

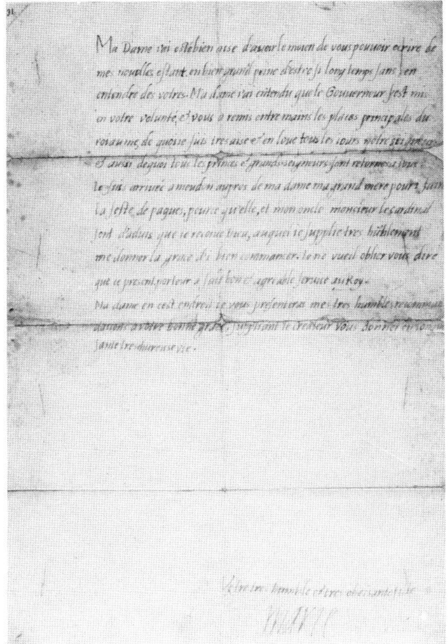

Ma Dame i'ai esté bien aise d'avoir le moien de vous pouvoir escrire de mes nouvelles estant en bien grand peine d'estre si long temps sans en entendre des votres. Ma dame i'ai entendu que le Gouverneur s'est mis en votre volunté et vous a remis entre mains les places principales du roiaume de quoi ie suis tres aise et en loue tous les iours notre [illegible] et aussi de quoi tous les princes et grands seigneurs sont retournés [illegible] le [illegible] arrivé a meudon aupres de ma dame ma grand mere pour i faire la feste de pasques, pource qu'elle, et mon oncle monsieur le cardinal sont d'advis que ie recoive Dieu, auquel ie supplie tres humblement me donner la grace d'i bien commancer. Ie ne veul oblier vous dire que ce present porteur a fait bon et agreable service au Roy.

Ma dame en cest endroit ie vous presenterai mes tres humbles recommandations a votre bonne grace, suppliant le createur vous donner en santé tres heureuse vie.

Votre tres humble et tres obeissante fille

MARIE

38. Letter written by Mary to her mother, when she was about eleven, commenting on the political news from Scotland and mentioning that she is spending Easter with her grandmother. (National Library of Scotland)

Mother herself. Be that as it might, there was every indication, she believed, that when the time came Mary would exercise power well, for she was quick-witted and able. She could hold her own in conversation with anyone. Henry II on one occasion thought fit to converse with her for a whole hour, and her uncle the Cardinal remarked admiringly when she was ten that already she was able to discourse like a woman of twenty-five.

Her relatives seized with delight upon every evidence of her growing maturity, for to them each day brought closer the time when she would be ready for marriage. Indeed they were becoming increasingly impatient. There was one nasty moment when it seemed that Henry II, for reasons of international politics, was having second thoughts about marrying his son to the Queen of Scots. Mercifully that crisis passed and he went back to treating her as his future daughter-in-law, but her friends remained nervous about his intentions and whenever they could, Mary's uncles dropped discreet hints that she was now mature enough for matrimony. The Dauphin, of course, would not legally be of age to wed until his fourteenth birthday in 1558, but the Guises would have liked some formal ceremony before that.

Henry II was well aware of their ambitions, but he was equally determined that he would not commit himself a moment too soon. As their enemies were always pointing out, this match would have the effect of raising the Guise family to undue prominence at Court, and there were those who argued that the Scottish alliance was more of a liability than an asset, a constant drain on resources with nothing coming back in return. Henry therefore had no intention of hurrying into the final commitment to Scotland. Not until October 1557 did he at last make up his mind. Because of recent changes on the international scene, the Scottish alliance had become vital once more.

39. *The Dauphin Francis*, aged about fourteen, by François Clouet. (The Bibliothèque Nationale, Paris)

At his request, nine Scottish commissioners, led by Mary's half-brother Lord James Stewart, arrived to negotiate the marriage contract and by the middle of April the terms had been hammered out. Henceforth Scotland and France would be united. Both Scots and French would have dual nationality, but various guarantees were written in, on the insistence of the Scots. Mary promised to preserve her country's ancient freedoms and privileges, and Henry agreed that if Francis died she would have the choice of staying in France or returning to her native land. If she herself died without having any children, he promised that he would uphold the rights of the next legal heir to her throne, the Earl of Arran.

On 11 April, Mary and the Dauphin were ceremoniously betrothed in the Great Hall of the Louvre, at that time one of the royal palaces. Triumphantly, Mary's uncle the Cardinal joined the hands of the young couple: his niece, a tall, willowy fifteen-year-old and the Dauphin, still undersized, pale, sullen and resentful of almost everyone but her. Afterwards, there was a lavish ball to celebrate the beginning of the new era.

40. *Mary, Queen of Scots*, aged about sixteen, by François Clouet. (The Bibliothèque Nationale, Paris)

Even as they joined in the rejoicings, however, the Scottish commissioners felt uneasy about the commitments they had just made and they would have been acutely alarmed had they known that the

formal agreement they had so painstakingly negotiated was accompanied by another, secret arrangement of a disturbingly sinister nature. The public terms of the treaty did not go far enough for Henry and his advisers. For all he might pretend otherwise, the King was merely using the Scots for his own purposes and so he told Mary that she must agree to another set of arrangements which would never be made public.

Regardless of anything she might sign in her marriage contract, she was to promise that if she died childless her kingdom would pass to Henry II, not to the nearest Scottish heir, and Henry would also inherit her rights to the English throne. Moreover, he would then be entitled to extract from the Scots enough money to pay the expenses he had incurred defending them from the English.

Mary was not naively unaware of what she was doing when she put her name to the secret terms. She had lived long enough at a sophisticated Court to appreciate the realities of politics. If she did not sign the agreement, there would be no marriage. The whole question of bequeathing her kingdom was in any case hypothetical, as she had no intention of dying without children. Accordingly, she signed the secret papers and prepared for her wedding with apparently no qualms of conscience.

41. Notre Dame Cathedral, Paris, where Mary was married. (French Government Tourist Office)

42. *The Dauphin Francis,* an engraving made to commemorate his marriage. (Scottish National Portrait Gallery)

43. *Mary, Queen of Scots,* an engraving made to commemorate her marriage. (Scottish National Portrait Gallery)

On Sunday, 24 April 1558, the people of Paris thronged the streets, eager to witness the festivities. The marriage ceremony was to take place at the Cathedral of Notre Dame, and the magnificent procession passed slowly between the jostling crowds. A contingent of colourfully dressed Swiss Guards led the way for Mary's eldest uncle, Francis, now Duke of Guise, and everyone pushed forward to wave and cheer as he went by. The air was filled with shouting and music, for trumpeters, drummers and fiddlers accompanied the procession. There were noblemen in jewelled satins and velvets, churchmen in exquisitely embroidered vestments and servants in scarlet and yellow. Following behind, came the small figure of the bridegroom almost weighed down by his magnificent garments, his two small brothers trotting at his side.

Finally, along came the procession everyone had been waiting for, and a gasp of amazement and appreciation ran through the spectators as they saw the bride. The Queen of Scots was all in white. No one had expected that, for in France white was the traditional mourning colour for a Queen and royal ladies normally chose cloth of gold or silver, or purple velvet for their wedding day.

Not so Mary. Her dazzling dress was of sumptuous material and, because she was a Queen, it had an unusually long train, carried by two small attendants. On her head was a gold crown set with enormous sapphires, rubies and pearls, and round her neck was a superb diamond necklace, its stones flashing whenever they caught the light. With her tall figure and her proud bearing, she impressed everyone who saw her as she paced slowly along, escorted by the King himself. Behind her, in second place for once, walked Catherine de Medici and the Princesses.

Gradually, Mary's procession wound its way towards the Cathedral and came to a halt outside in an area surrounded by specially erected

44. *George, 5th Lord Seton,* Master of the Household to Mary, carrying his baton of office, by an unknown artist.
(National Gallery of Scotland, on loan to the Scottish National Portrait Gallery)

stands. In the Middle Ages, weddings took place outside the church, at its doors, and this was the pattern being followed that day. In the open air, surrounded by all the dignitaries of the French Court and many foreign ambassadors, the Archbishop of Rouen performed the wedding ceremony, and, when the couple exchanged their promises, Henry II drew off one of his own rings and passed it to the Dauphin, who then placed it on the finger of his bride. The congregation moved into the Cathedral after that, to hear Mass, before emerging into the daylight once more, Mary and her uncles towering over the Dauphin and the other royal children.

During the festivities which followed, the Guises felt an enormous sense of relief. Up to the very last moment, their enemies had been saying that the marriage would never take place, and the King of Navarre, who was one of the guests, had been heard to murmur to the Venetian ambassador, 'Thou seest the conclusion of a fact which very few credited till now'. The uncertainty was over at last, their dearest ambition had been realised, and their niece was safely married. The enemies of the house of Guise had been routed. They could look forward to a glorious future for themselves and, of course, for their niece, the Queen Dauphiness.

The wedding celebrations began with a lavish banquet and continued throughout the evening with a grand ball. Finally, the high point of the day came when the bride and groom were put to bed by the royal family and the principal guests. This was a traditional part of the ceremonial, and it usually took place amidst a good deal of ribald teasing. On this occasion, there were those who shook their heads and murmured to each other that Francis was still a child and likely to remain so, but if the prayers of the King and Queen were answered, time would remedy that.

The light-hearted atmosphere of rejoicing lasted throughout the summer, until it was marred by an unexpected tragedy. The nine Scottish ambassadors set off for home in September, but on the way they were

45. Mary and the Dauphin, a heraldic drawing from the Scottish Forman Armorial of the 1560s.
(National Library of Scotland)

taken violently ill and four of them died, probably of food poisoning. To the Scots, their death seemed to be an ill omen, and later that autumn it seemed that their worst fears were being confirmed when Henry II wrote demanding that the Scottish crown be sent over to France so that the Dauphin could be crowned King of Scots.

It had certainly been agreed that Francis should have the crown matrimonial during the marriage, that is to say, that he would rule jointly with Mary, and in keeping with this arrangement official documents now went out under the names of 'Francis and Mary, King and Queen of Scots' but the Scots could not contemplate parting with such a precious symbol of their country's nationhood. On the other hand, they were not in a position to give Henry an outright refusal, so they delayed and delayed and in the end the crown never did leave the country.

46. *Mary, Queen of Scots,* engraved from a medallion of 1559. (Scottish National Portrait Gallery)

In the meantime, Mary, Queen of Scots was settling down to her altered status. In practice, her marriage brought about very little change to her way of life, except that she and the Dauphin now shared the same household and she was also spending an increasing amount of time with her mother-in-law. The two Queens had little in common, for they were as different in disposition as they were in appearance. Mary was almost six feet tall now, and with her creamy white skin, her auburn hair and her fascinating, narrow brown eyes she was much praised as the leading beauty of the Court. By comparison, Catherine de Medici was not only a generation older; she was squat, dark and unprepossessing. While Mary's warmth and openness endeared her to all who knew her, Catherine had a reputation for malice and scheming. Many people had speculated about how the two women would get on together now that the

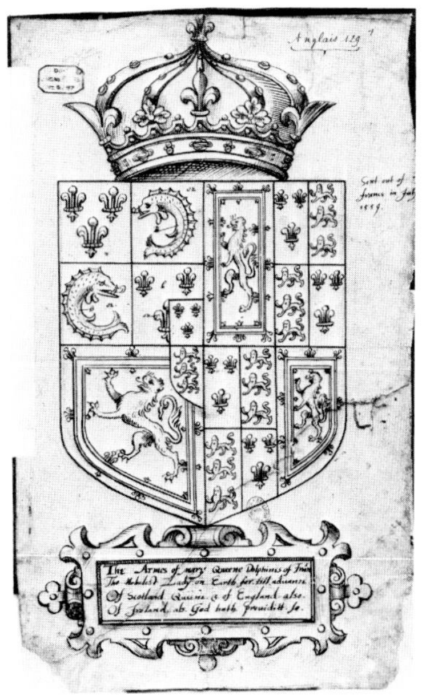

47. Coat of arms of Mary, showing the arms of England quartered with those of Scotland and France.
(The Bibliothèque Nationale, Paris)

Queen of Scots had grown up, but instead of quarrelling they were completely united by a shared preoccupation: the well-being of the Dauphin.

Had Mary and Francis been passionately in love with each other, Catherine would undoubtedly have been consumed with jealousy, but as it was she knew that Mary's attitude towards the boy was that of an affectionate, protective elder sister, and she could see that her daughter-in-law was positively good for him. Together she and Mary discussed his health, worried about his many ailments and seized gladly upon any sign, however slight, that he was growing to manhood. One day, Francis would rule over his people as God's representative on earth. It was firmly believed in French royal circles that the monarch was divinely chosen and responsible to God alone for the welfare of his subjects and so Mary grew up convinced that she and her husband were set apart from everyone by their central and mystical role in society. Moreover, her sense of her own important destiny was increased when her father-in-law announced that she and Francis were also the rightful monarchs of England as well as Scotland.

That winter, Elizabeth Tudor had succeeded to the throne of England, thin, clever, red-haired Elizabeth, flirtatious, unpredictable and wary. She was Mary's cousin: the daughter of Henry VIII and his second wife, but she had been born while his first wife was still alive and in the eyes of the Roman Catholic Church she was illegitimate. That being so, Catholics believed that she had no right to the English throne and instead Mary, Queen of Scots seemed the most likely candidate for she was descended from Henry VIII's sister. The French King therefore issued his proclamation and, within a scandalously short time, Mary's royal canopy, her banners and her silver plate all appeared bearing the arms of England quartered with those of Scotland and France.

48. The tournament at which Henry II was fatally injured: an engraving. (The Bibliothèque Nationale, Paris)

The English ambassador was beside himself with rage, but Henry II was not in a position to enforce Mary's claim and it was generally agreed that a period of peace was necessary so that the countries of Western Europe could work out their new alignments, Accordingly, France, Spain and England signed the Treaty of Câteau-Cambrésis in April 1559. As usual, several marriages were arranged and by one of these Mary's childhood friend, Princess Elisabeth, was betrothed to Philip II of Spain.

Philip decided not to come in person to claim his latest bride, and so instead a proxy wedding was arranged. It would take place in June and Henry II, an enthusiastic jouster, arranged a series of celebratory tournaments. Clad in black and white, the favourite colours of his mistress, Diane de Poitiers, he rode three times at the lists.

As his third opponent thundered towards him, disaster struck. The unfortunate nobleman, Jacques de Lorges, thrust forward his lance. At the moment of impact it shattered, splinters lodging in Henry's eye and his neck. Mortally wounded, he was carried into a nearby house. For ten days he lay unmoving, attended by all his family including Mary, Queen of Scots, and then he died. The Dauphin in that moment became King of France, and Mary's uncles seized their opportunity. They would rule on his behalf.

In the emergency, Mary was ready to play her own part. The dead King's family were completely demoralised, and they turned to her for comfort and support. It was she who tried to console Catherine de Medici, and, when the Spanish ambassador arrived to present Philip II's condolences, it was Mary who made a suitable reply to his speech while Catherine sat at her side, too overcome to speak. It was Mary, too, who gave orders that the late King's jewels should be listed, so that those which he had illegally lavished upon Diane de Poitiers could be reclaimed. As the new Queen of France, Mary would require them herself.

Henry II was buried at St Denis and then in September the Dauphin was crowned at Rheims. He was still unready for the new responsibilities. As Mary herself remarked, he seemed entirely obedient to his mother and he

49. The death of Henry II: Mary is one of the figures at his bedside in this engraving.
(The Bibliothèque Nationale, Paris)

50. Rheims Cathedral, where Francis II was crowned.
(French Government Tourist Office)

51. Rheims Cathedral, interior.
(French Government Tourist Office)

continued to behave like a slow-witted child. Despite his precarious health, he had developed a passion for hunting, and it seemed that nothing else could hold his attention. He moved from one palace to the next in pursuit of this sport, with the result that he neglected affairs of state for days on end. When he was persuaded to look at papers and listen to the complicated explanations of the Duke of Guise and the Cardinal of Lorraine, he did so with an apathy which even the most tolerant found irritating.

Mary herself was increasingly preoccupied with the news from Scotland, for it had soon become clear that the Protestants there had found a willing new ally in Elizabeth of England. On 27 February 1560, the English Queen signed the Treaty of Berwick, promising to come to the assistance of Lord James and the others who were rebelling against Mary of Guise, and thereafter an English army marched north and besieged Leith. Worn out by her long years of unremitting struggle, the Queen Mother died in Edinburgh Castle on 11 June.

Mary, Queen of Scots was inconsolable but the situation in Scotland had to be resolved somehow, and after protracted negotiations the Treaty of Edinburgh was signed on 6 July. By its terms, both the English and French armies would withdraw from Scotland, each leaving only sixty of their men behind. It was also agreed that Francis II and Mary would now recognise Elizabeth as rightful Queen of England by ceasing to quarter the English arms with their own.

That August, the Scottish Lords regularised their religious situation. Parliament passed a series of acts authorising a new Protestant Confession of Faith, abolishing the Pope's jurisdiction over Scotland and making both the saying and the hearing of Mass illegal. Scotland was indeed being ruled by its Protestant nobility.

The French could not allow that state of affairs to continue for long, but before they could take any action to replace Mary of Guise with a Regent of their own choosing, a fresh tragedy intervened. One day in November, Francis came back from a day's hunting, complaining of a violent pain in his ear. At first, no one was unduly alarmed. He always had been troubled with earache and no doubt the bitterly cold wind was responsible. However, he fainted next evening at Vespers and soon he was in the grip of a raging fever. The entire Court was thrown into a panic, and Mary and Catherine de Medici refused to move from his bedside, nursing him with tender care. In spite of their efforts, the ear infection developed into an abcess on the brain and on 5 December 1560 he died. With his death, Mary lost not only the adoring companion of her childhood, but her position as Queen of France. Her uncles could no longer claim supreme power, and instead Catherine de Medici became Regent of France, ruling on behalf of her next son, Charles IX.

The Queen of Scots put on her white royal mourning and, as etiquette demanded, she shut herself away in a darkened chamber hung with black. There she would have to spend forty days, attended only by her immediate family. Her grandmother and her uncles did their best to offer consolation, but she wept uncontrollably. She had worn herself out, said the English ambassador, 'by long watching with him during his sickness and painful diligence about him'. 'Her unhappiness and her incessant tears call forth general compassion,' said another member of the diplomatic community.

For the rest of her life, Mary regarded Francis II as her true husband, the partner chosen for her by God, and throughout all her later troubles she

52. *Mary, Queen of Scots,* a bust by Ponce Jacquio, about 1560. (Scottish National Portrait Gallery)

treasured mementoes of him and of her life as his consort. Already shaken by the loss of her mother, she could hardly believe that he was gone too and, as she wrote in a poem lamenting his death, she felt his presence at her side wherever she was: 'At work or at rest, he is always near me'.

Her relatives sought to distract her thoughts by reminding her that she must make a decision about her future, and indeed it was now a matter of some urgency. By her marriage contract, she was free to remain in France, or she could return to Scotland. More important still, she was once more eligible for marriage and before Francis was even dead, people had been speculating about a new husband for her. Within a fortnight of Francis's end, it was noticed that Mary was no longer observing the strict seclusion of her mourning chamber. Ambassadors, bishops and diplomats were seen entering, then emerging again after what were obviously lengthy discussions.

There were, in fact, many candidates for her hand, as almost every eligible man in Europe assessed his own chances and sent off representatives to woo the Queen. Some were too poor or too lowly to merit consideration. Others had sufficient prestige and wealth to make them serious contenders, but it did not take Mary long to make up her mind. What she wanted to do was to marry the heir to the throne of Spain, Don Carlos.

He did have his disadvantages, of course, which the Spanish diplomats did their best to conceal. Now sixteen years old, he still weighed less than six stones and, as well as having misshapen shoulders and a speech impediment, he suffered from epilepsy. If Francis II had been delicate and undersized, he would have seemed positively robust compared with Don Carlos. However, he possessed near kingly status, combined with wealth. The very day after the death of Francis, the English envoy in France had told Queen Elizabeth that Mary's greatest concern was the continuation of her honour. According to him, she would marry 'one that may uphold her to be great' rather than someone who merely pleased her fancy. In this judgment he was perfectly correct. Foreign ambassadors might prattle about the relative merits of the King of Denmark or the Archduke of Austria, but Mary had set her heart on becoming the bride of Don Carlos.

It was far too early to make public her ambition, of course, hence her secret discussions with her uncles and the Spanish ambassador. In spite of all their precautions, however, Catherine de Medici found out, and she was furious. Mary must not be allowed to make this dazzling match which would place her at the forefront of European affairs and give Spain a dangerously useful ally. Apart from that, if Mary married Don Carlos she would soon outshine the King of Spain's wife, and she, of course, was Catherine's daughter Elisabeth.

This was no idle fear on Catherine's part. Foreign ambassadors were already noticing that there was far more to the Queen of Scots than they had previously imagined. During the lifetime of Francis II they had paid little attention to her because, like any other wife, she was 'under the subjection' of her husband. Now, though, the English ambassador reported that 'she is both of great wisdom for her years, modesty and also of great judgment in the wise handling of herself and her matters,' and he concluded that 'some, such as made no great account of her, do now, seeing her wisdom, both honour and pity her'. It was obvious to them all that the jealous Catherine would do her best to keep Mary in the background, and her life as Queen Dowager would not be an enviable one.

At Catherine's instigation, her daughter Elisabeth therefore reminded Philip II that by taking Mary as his daughter-in-law he would be committing himself to a costly military campaign in Scotland. Was that what he really wanted? It was not, and in the spring of 1561 he let it be known that there would be no marriage for Mary with his son.

She was bitterly disappointed. Where else was she to find a partner equal to her in status? If circumstances had been different she could have

53. *Charles IX, King of France*, Mary's brother-in-law, by an unknown artist. (The Bibliothèque Nationale, Paris)

54. *Francis, Duke of Guise*, Mary's uncle, engraved from a portrait painted towards the end of his life. (Scottish National Portrait Gallery)

retained her position as Queen of France by marrying her brother-in-law Charles IX, but Catherine would never allow that. No other suitor possessed the resources of France or Spain, and so her thoughts began to turn in a different direction altogether. She decided that she would go back to Scotland.

Her friends were horrified and they warned her bluntly that she could not return unless she went at the head of an army which would drive out the Protestant Lords and place her on the throne. In recent weeks, however, Lord James Stewart and the Scots had actually invited her back and the more she discussed it with envoys sent to her by her parliament, the more attractive did the prospect seem. She would govern as she had been born to do, she would bring the Scots back to their obedience to their rightful monarch and the true religion, and best of all she would do as she chose herself, with no Catherine de Medici to interfere.

That spring she went to visit her Guise relatives in north-east France and while she was there Lord James arrived in person to see her. He was thirty now, to her eighteen, an able, experienced man who was royal in all but name. Indeed, except for the accident of birth, he would have inherited the Scottish throne instead of her. Since that was not possible, his father had intended him for a career in the Catholic Church, but his ambitions lay elsewhere and with the Reformation he became a convinced Protestant. In some ways Mary found him stern and humourless, but she respected his integrity and she felt that they could work out a compromise.

Even when he began their conversation by asking her to renounce her Catholicism in favour of the Protestant religion, she was not too

55. Drawing of Mary, in white mourning, by François Clouet. (The Bibliothèque Nationale, Paris)

dismayed, for she had expected no less. She refused point blank, and replied with a smile that, if he would return to the Catholic faith, she would see to it that he became a Cardinal. His refusal was as instant as hers had been, and after that, the preliminary skirmishing over, they settled down to a serious discussion.

In spite of Mary's very real devotion to the Catholic religion, she was prepared to be adaptable. Like a significant number of French Catholics, she believed that by marching against Protestants with an army, a monarch was simply encouraging strife. Tolerance should be tried instead. It was worth allowing other modes of worship if that kept the peace and then, in time, people could be shown their error. She therefore told Lord James that she was willing to return, so long as she was allowed to attend Catholic services in private. He agreed, advising her that she should recognise the Protestant Church. On that basis they were able to proceed and her future was decided. By her own choice alone, she would go back.

At the beginning of June, she went to Paris to make the final arrangements for her departure and she sent a request to Queen Elizabeth for a safe conduct. This should have been no more than a formality, but Elizabeth flew into a rage and told her emissary that she was not interested in safe conducts. What she wanted to know was, had Mary ratified the Treaty of Edinburgh recognising Elizabeth as Queen? The envoy had to admit that she had not, whereupon Elizabeth curtly refused to grant the pass.

56. Painting of Mary, in white mourning, by François Clouet; said to be Elizabeth Tudor's favourite picture of her cousin. (Reproduced by gracious permission of Her Majesty The Queen)

ELEGIE SVR LE DES-
part de la Royne Marie retour-
nant à ſon Royaume
d'Eſcoſſe.

OMME vn beau pré
deſpouillé de ſes fleurs,
Comme vn tableau priué
de ſes couleurs,
Comme le ciel s'il perdoit
ſes eſtoilles,
La mer ſes eaues: le nauire ſes voiles,
Comme vn beau champ de ſon bled deſ-
couuert,
Et cõme vn bois perdãt ſon mãteau verd,
Et vn anneau ſa pierre precieuſe,
Ainſi perdra la France ſoucieuſe
Ses ornemens en perdant la beauté
Qui fut ſa fleur, ſa couleur & clarté.
Dure fortune indomptable & felonne
Tu es vrayement fille d'vne Lyonne,
Tu vas paſſant les Tygres en rigueur:

A 2

57. Poem by Pierre de Ronsard, lamenting Mary's departure from France, 1561. (National Library of Scotland)

Mary was both surprised and indignant when she heard what had happened, and next time the English ambassador, Sir Nicholas Throckmorton called upon her, she raised her voice so that everyone in the chamber could hear, and invited him pleasantly to come to one side with her. It would be best if they spoke a little apart from their companions, she said loudly, for it would never do if he said something to annoy her and she gave an exhibition of petulance and ill-temper. Her meaning was not lost on any of those present.

In a subsequent interview with Throckmorton, she laid irony aside and said in her accustomed, straightforward manner,

'Monsieur l'Ambassadeur, if my preparations were not so well advanced as they are, perhaps the Queen your mistress's unkindness might stop my voyage, but now I am determined to adventure the matter, whatsoever comes of it. I trust the wind will be so favourable as I shall not need to come to the coast of England, but if I do, then Monsieur l'Ambassadeur, the Queen your mistress shall have me in her hands to do her will of me, and if she be so hard-hearted as to desire my end, she may then do her pleasure and make sacrifice of me.' Always fond of a dramatic turn of phrase, she added, 'Perhaps that eventuality might be better for me than to live: but in this matter, God's will be done!'

Four days later, on 25 July 1561 she said goodbye to Catherine de Medici and Charles IX and set off for the coast. Six of her uncles travelled with her. She had sent further requests to Elizabeth, but by mid-August no safe conduct had come and she decided that she could wait no longer. On 14 August she embarked on board the great white galley which was to carry her to Scotland. With her went three of her uncles and a retinue of friends and attendants, including the faithful four Maries. The Duke of Guise and the Cardinal of Lorraine did not dare leave France for a lengthy period for fear of what Catherine de Medici might do in their absence, but they were on the quayside to see their niece off. The Cardinal, always practical, interrupted his farewell speech to suggest that Mary should leave her dazzling collection of jewels with him, for safety. Mary looked at him with affectionate amusement. If he was willing to trust her to the high seas, she said, then surely her valuables would be safe too.

Her ready wit had not deserted her at the moment of parting, but her mood was not light-hearted. For all that it was summertime, the sky was grey and a thick mist hung above the water. As her great galley drew slowly away from the shore and the cliffs of Calais receded into the haze, the Queen realised for the first time the enormity of what she was doing, and she wept.

'Adieu, France. Adieu, dear France,' she murmured brokenly. 'I fear I shall never see you again.'

3

THE QUEEN OF SCOTS

THE QUEEN'S travelling companions, nervous of being intercepted by the English, were more concerned about the voyage itself than they were about leaving France, and there was considerable alarm when some of Elizabeth's ships were sighted, bearing down on the royal fleet as they sailed up the east coast of England. For a moment, it seemed as though their worst fears were to be realised. Had Elizabeth decided to seize her cousin and prevent her from returning to her kingdom? Was that why she had refused to grant the safe conduct? They waited with bated breath, but the enemy vessels did not come any closer to the galleys. They merely saluted and allowed them to pass, though they did insist on searching the accompanying vessels, on the pretext of looking for pirates. Elizabeth had simply wanted to make a show of strength, it seemed. On this occasion, her ships posed no threat and with many a sigh of relief the French party continued on its way north.

On 18 August, local people at Flamborough Head saw the two great galleys sailing so close in to the shore that they could make out the colour of the ships, one white, the other red, and they could see that each flew two flags. A blue flag bore the French royal arms on it and the second flag, which was white, glistened like silver when the summer sun pierced the haze. Early next day, the convoy entered the Firth of Forth and, about nine o'clock in the morning the vessels sailed into Leith harbour, fired off their guns in greeting and dropped their anchors.

Excitedly, the Queen and her friends prepared to disembark. Leith was Edinburgh's port, a bustling town filled with activity, but their first glimpse of it that day was hardly encouraging. The mist had thickened into the dense sea fog which often affects that part of Scotland's east coast in August and, to make matters worse, there was no sign of any official welcoming party waiting on the quayside. The Scots were well aware that their Queen was coming, but they had not expected her so soon. The noise of the cannons booming had brought out groups of curious townspeople and they stood transfixed when they saw the royal party descend from the galley: the Queen, a tall, dramatic figure in her mourning clothes, followed by a group of richly dressed courtiers led by her tall Guise uncles.

The local dignitaries came hurrying out to meet her and, at a loss to know what to do in the absence of the Lords, they ushered her into the house of Andrew Lamb, a wealthy local merchant. There, she and her party could rest for a little, recover from the rigours of the voyage and take some refreshment, while messengers rode urgently up to Edinburgh to tell Lord James and the other courtiers that the Queen had come home.

By early afternoon the nobility had gathered at Andrew Lamb's house, Mary had eaten dinner, and her welcome proper could begin. She came out on to the street to the excited cheering of the populace and, escorted by her nobles, she travelled the short distance to the palace of

58. Mary, about 1561, by an artist of the school of Clouet.
(Musée Condé, Chantilly: photograph, Giraudon)

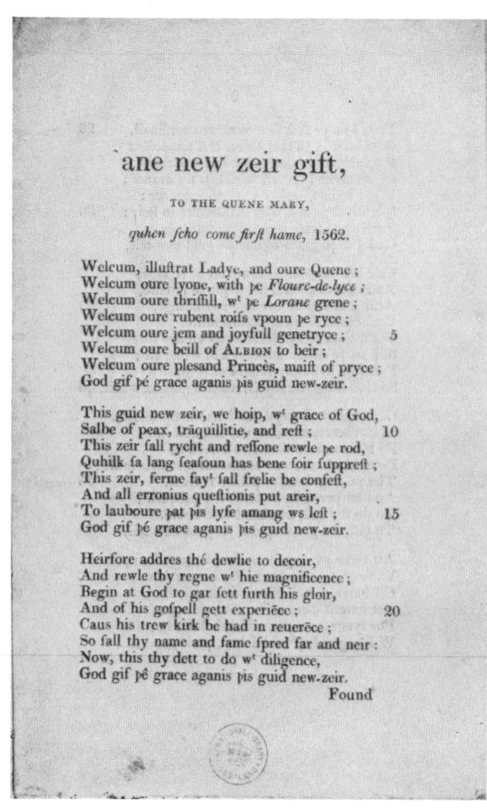

ane new zeir gift,

TO THE QUENE MARY,

quhen ſcho come firſt hame, 1562.

Welcum, illuſtrat Ladye, and oure Quene ;
Welcum oure lyone, with þe *Floure-de-lyce* ;
Welcum oure thriſſill, wᵗ þe *Lorane* grene ;
Welcum oure rubent roiſs vpoun þe ryce ;
Welcum oure jem and joyfull genetryce ;
Welcum oure beill of ALBION to beir ;
Welcum oure plesand Princès, maiſt of pryce ;
God gif þé grace aganis þis guid new-zeir.

This guid new zeir, we hoip, wᵗ grace of God,
Salbe of peax, trāquillitie, and reſt ;
This zeir ſall rycht and reſſone rewle þe rod,
Quhilk ſa lang ſeaſoun has bene ſoir ſuppreſt ;
This zeir, ferme fayᵗ ſall frelie be confeſt,
And all erronius queſtionis put areir,
To lauboure þat þis lyſe amang ws leſt ;
God gif þé grace aganis þis guid new-zeir.

Heirfore addres thé dewlie to decoir,
And rewle thy regne wᵗ hie magnificence ;
Begin at God to gar ſett furth his gloir,
And of his goſpell gett experiēce ;
Caus his trew kirk be had in reuerēce ;
So ſall thy name and fame ſpred far and neir :
Now, this thy dett to do wᵗ diligence,
God gif þê grace aganis þis guid new-zeir.

Found

59. Poem by Alexander Scott, welcoming Mary back to Scotland, 1561. (National Library of Scotland)

Holyroodhouse. Everywhere she looked there were crowds of excited bystanders, for it seemed that the entire population had turned out to see her. Dull though the weather was, the whole atmosphere had been transformed into one of spontaneous rejoicing and even Mary's bitterest enemies had to admit that all who saw her were delighted with her. She was young, beautiful and charming and, elated by the unexpected warmth of her reception, she responded with laughter and vivacity to the crowds who pressed round her. Accustomed as she had been to admiration and praise, she was in her element, convinced now that she had made the right decision in coming home. Her subjects were far more enthusiastic and friendly than she had been led to believe. There were scarcely any dour, sullen faces in the throng and she felt that day that it would not be so difficult, after all, to win her people back to their proper allegiance to her and to the Catholic Church.

Arriving at her palace of Holyroodhouse, a handsome, stone building set in the shadow of the hill called Arthur's Seat, she was taken up to her chambers in the north-west tower. This part of the palace had been built by her father, in the French style, so it was in no way strange to her and everyone she met seemed eager to make her feel at home. That night, the Edinburgh crowds came to serenade her, singing and playing musical instruments beneath her window. The French poet, Brantôme, who had travelled with her retinue, complained bitterly about what he called the doleful psalms and discordant noise, saying that they kept the Queen

60. *James, Earl of Moray,* Mary's half-brother, by Hans Eworth, 1561. (In a Scottish private collection)

awake. She herself was delighted, though, and she told her wellwishers that she had enjoyed the music so much she hoped it would be repeated. To Brantôme's disgust, they took her at her word and returned on several subsequent evenings.

Mary arrived in Scotland on a Tuesday and the mutual pleasure she and her subjects found in each other lasted until the following Sunday. On that day, the Queen attended Mass in the Chapel Royal at Holyrood, accompanied by her uncles and her own household. The priest was French too, but as soon as word leaked out there was an uproar. In a country which was newly Protestant, the celebration of Mass seemed like a deliberate, dangerous threat, an intentional challenge to the Reformers and their followers.

A small crowd quickly gathered in the forecourt at Holyrood and when they saw a servant hurrying across the courtyard towards the chapel, they attacked him, dashing from his hands the altar candlesticks he was carrying. Hearing the noise, Lord James appeared before any more damage was done and he stationed himself at the chapel door. A fervent

61. *Lady Agnes Keith, Countess of Moray*, by Hans Eworth, about 1561. (In a Scottish private collection)

Protestant he might be, but he had promised his half-sister that she should worship privately as she pleased, and he did not intend to break his word. At the sight of him, the angry mob fell back.

Inside, the service proceeded more or less uninterrupted, although those present observed that the priest celebrating Mass trembled so much that he could hardly lift the chalice. When the service was over, two of Mary's other Scottish half-brothers, Lord John and Lord Robert, gave him their protection, walking back with him to his chamber. That evening, large numbers of people came down to Holyrood to demonstrate their discontent.

The next day, Mary made her first real move as Queen, by issuing a proclamation. With the advice of her parliament she would, she said, settle the religion of her kingdom soon, but in the meantime there would be no change. The Scots could attend their Protestant sermons, but in return she expected to worship as she chose and no one was to bother or attack her servants.

62. Coat of arms of the Earl of Moray, crossed by the bar sinister, showing that he was illegitimate: from the Forman Armorial. (National Library of Scotland)

This appeared to satisfy most of her Lords, but far from being placated was the Protestant preacher, John Knox, and he exercised considerable influence. Originally a Catholic priest, he had become a friend of George Wishart and a follower of the doctrines of John Calvin. Mary knew all about him, for he had been a thorn in her mother's flesh for years, and, even before she had left France she told friends that she was determined to banish him from the kingdom. Now, on 31 August, he preached a powerful sermon, condemning the Mass and Mary's private services.

Two day later, the Queen was formally welcomed to her capital city. She dined that Tuesday in Edinburgh Castle, and afterwards she made a stately progress back to Holyroodhouse. As she moved slowly down the Castle Hill beneath a purple canopy fringed with gold, fifty young men disguised as Moors capered along in front of her. Their faces were hidden by black masks, on their heads they wore black caps and their yellow taffeta suits were hung about with glittering gold chains. The fountain at the Market Cross flowed with wine, maidens in diaphanous dresses posed as the Virtues, and various mythological and religious episodes were re-enacted: a dragon was ceremoniously slaughtered at the Nether Bow and at the Salt Tron three Old Testament characters were apparently burned to death.

The Castle cannon fired a salute, boys and girls made pretty speeches, there was singing and there was cheering, but even on this happy occasion an undercurrent of discontent disturbed the Queen and her

63. *John Knox the Reformer,* from a woodcut believed to be the only authentic likeness of him. (Scottish National Portrait Gallery)

9

THE FIRST BLAST
TO AWAKE WOMEN
degenerate.

O promote a woman to beare rule, ſuperioritie, dominion or empire aboue any realme, nation, or citie, is repugnãt to nature, cõtumelie to God, a thing moſt contrarious to his reueled will and approued ordinãce, and finallie it is the ſubuerſion of good order, of all equitie and iuſtice.

In the probation of this propoſition, I will not be ſo curious, as to gather what ſoeuer may amplifie, ſet furth, or decore the ſame, but I am purpoſed, euen as I haue ſpoken my conſcience in moſt plaine ãd fewe wordes, ſo to ſtãd content with a ſimple proofe of euerie membre, bringing in for my witneſſe Goddes ordinance in nature, his plaine will reueled in his worde, and the mindes of ſuch as be moſte auncient amongeſt godlie writers.

And firſt, where that I affirme the em-

B i

64. The opening lines of Knox's famous book, *The First Blast of the Trumpet against the Monstrous Regiment of Women.* (National Library of Scotland)

retinue. There was talk that the people at the Salt Tron had really intended burning an effigy of a priest and had only changed their plans at the last minute when the Catholic Earl of Huntly stopped them. Less dramatically, but with just as much significance, when a child came down from a painted cloud at the Butter Tron and presented the Queen with the keys of Edinburgh, he also handed her two books covered in rich purple velvet. One was the Bible, in English instead of Latin, and the other was the Protestant Service Book, unmistakable symbols, both of them, of the Reformed religion.

Although the Queen smiled and remained calmly unperturbed at the time, she was angry and she decided to rebuke the person who was responsible for these unseemly additions to the pageantry. She was in no doubt about his identity. She summoned John Knox to Holyrood and, that Thursday morning, they met face to face for the first time. Knox has left an account of what passed between them that day, and although his description is obviously biased, it gives a very clear picture of events.

The audience was a private one. The only other people there were Lord James, who stood a little to one side and was obviously to take no part in the proceedings, and two of the Queen's ladies, who were seated at the far end of the room. Finally confronting the man who had caused her mother so much trouble and pain, Mary immediately accused Knox of inciting her subjects to rebel against their rightful monarch. It was clear from what she said that she was not so much concerned with the religious issues as with the problem of civil disorder. She had encountered Protestants before and she believed that they fell into two categories: the agitators who deliberately stirred up the populace to challenge the rightful authority of the ruler, and the people themselves, honest subjects, led into error by evil-intentioned men. God enjoined men and women to obey their princes. It was the duty of the ruler to keep them in the right ways and so the actions of men like Knox roused in her a genuine indignation. She therefore made a spirited speech, telling him that he must submit to his monarch and stop stirring up strife.

Knox heard her out, and then he replied baldly that subjects should not obey a monarch who was ungodly. If a father became mad, he said, and threatened to kill his children, it was their duty to restrain him. In the same way, when subjects found themselves being ruled by a Catholic, it was their duty to disobey him because he was dangerously wrong.

Mary could hardly believe her ears. She had never been exposed to such blatant rudeness before. What subject ever had the temerity to speak like that to his prince? According to Knox, she 'stood as if amazed, more than a quarter of an hour' without speaking. It was not simply amazement which kept her silent, though. She could hardly trust herself to speak and Lord James, reading her expression more accurately than Knox had done, came over and asked her what had offended her.

'Well,' she said at last to Knox, when she had herself in hand, 'then I perceive that my subjects shall obey you and not me, and shall do what they wish and not what I command, and so must I be subject to them and not they to me!'

'God forbid', retorted Knox, that he should ever command anyone to

65. Knox haranguing Mary: an imaginary drawing done in the 1560s, from *An Oration against the Unlawful Insurrections* by P. Frarinus. (The Trustees of the British Library)

obey him; but everyone, Kings and Queens alike, was subject to God's will. He then embarked upon a lengthy and extremely complicated series of theological arguments, haranguing Mary in a tone which verged on the downright insulting. When at last he had finished, she looked at him and said sardonically, 'Ye are ower sair for me,' meaning that his arguments were too difficult for her, and she wished aloud that she had learned Catholic advisers with her to argue with him on his own terms. She could not debate his technical points so instead she put forward her own honest opinions, the beliefs she had accepted since childhood. The Catholic Church was for her the true church and the monarch of a country was appointed by God. They talked themselves hoarse but in the end all they knew was that there could never be any understanding between them. Eventually their conversation was interrupted by an obliging courtier who came to announce that the Queen's dinner was ready, and she thankfully brought the interview to an end.

When Knox emerged from the palace, his friends were waiting eagerly to hear all about his meeting. What was Mary like? What did he think of her? He was only too ready to tell them.

'If there be not in her a proud mind, a crafty wit and an indurate heart against God and his truth,' he replied, 'my judgment faileth me'. In fact, he had seen only what he wanted to see, for he was determined to distrust her. He noted her charm and her beauty, and in his innermost heart he was afraid that she would somehow undermine his resolution. He believed he could recognise in her that very quality which he had identified in her mother—the mysterious fascination which could somehow win over the staunchest adversary. That, combined with her physical attractiveness, made her doubly dangerous.

'In communication with her I espied such craft as I have not found in such age,' he remarked some weeks later. Mary was a threat to his own authority over his followers and everyone must be warned against her. As an English emissary remarked,

'Mr Knox cannot be otherwise persuaded but that many men are deceived in this woman.'

The prospects for the future relationship between Queen and preacher were far from promising.

Disgusted by what she considered to be Knox's insolence, Mary was glad to turn her mind to more pleasant matters and she began to plan her first progress through her kingdom. She was eager to see and be seen by her subjects, and, since she did not particularly care for Edinburgh, she resolved to spend the second half of September visiting her principal towns and residences, spending about two days in each.

At the start, all went well. She began by travelling to Linlithgow, the place of her birth, then she moved west to Stirling Castle, which she may have remembered from childhood. The first signs of trouble came that Sunday when her priests celebrated High Mass in the Chapel Royal. Lord James, her former protector, became involved in some kind of disturbance in the choir and in the resulting scuffle several of the clergy present were said to have emerged with 'broken heads and bloody ears'.

That was upsetting enough, but worse was to follow. Perth was the next stopping place and as usual huge crowds of enthusiastic spectators turned out to see the Queen and enjoy the colourful processions. Mary was presented with a gold box in the shape of a heart, filled with gold coins, but the pageants put on for her were so obviously hostile to the Catholic Church that they caused her a great deal of distress and she fainted. She had to be carried from her horse to her lodgings nearby, suffering from the illness one observer said 'she is often troubled with, after any great unkindness or grief of mind'. However, she was able to travel to Dundee as planned, and then she went southwards to St Andrews, the ancient ecclesiastical capital of Scotland.

Her Sunday services there caused some minor trouble, but there were no major disturbances. After that, she spent a pleasant few days at Falkland Palace. This elegant building, much extended by her father, was a favourite hunting lodge of the Stewart kings and Mary admired it just as much as her predecessors had done. Regretfully, she had to leave at the end of the month and return to Edinburgh.

66. Falkland Palace, one of Mary's favourite residences: an aerial view. (National Trust for Scotland)

67. Falkland Palace.
(Photograph, Michael
Brooks)

68. Falkland Palace: the gatehouse, built for Mary's father.
(Photograph, Michael Brooks)

69. Falkland Palace: the south range, improved by Mary's father. (National Trust for Scotland)

70. Falkland Palace: the tennis court, built in 1539 for Mary's father. (National Trust for Scotland)

In her absence her opponents had been busy. Hardly had she arrived back, when Edinburgh Town Council issued a proclamation which was a calculated challenge to her authority. Provocative in tone, it ordered 'monks, friars, priests, nuns, adulterers, fornicators and all such filthy persons' to leave the capital immediately. Anyone who came into these categories and was within the burgh boundaries the next day would be seized, carted through the streets, branded and forcibly banished. Mary knew at once that this was aimed at her own French retinue and she was furious. She sent orders that the provost and bailies were to be replaced immediately and she issued her own counter-proclamation declaring that all her law-abiding citizens were perfectly free to move about the town as they pleased.

With that, the situation settled down into a somewhat uneasy peace. Despite Knox's fulminations, the Protestants were not about to rise and dispatch their Queen back to France. Indeed, most of them were still charmed with her. Wherever she went, the crowds reacted with enthusiasm for, apart from anything else, she made a striking figure in her rich, black dresses with their lace trimmings and their billowing skirts. She might still be in mourning for Francis II, but it was far from dowdy mourning. Her clothes were cut in the latest style and her hair was elaborately dressed with extra hair pieces. On ceremonial occasions she discarded her dark garments in favour of magnificent cloth of gold or silver and purple or crimson velvet, her jewels blazing in the light. Her collection of jewellery was breathtaking, from her fabulous black pearls to her gold chains and her ruby and emerald rings, many of them gifts from her first husband and his family. She was every inch a Queen, and she had inherited all the legendary Stewart charm.

Her father had been famous for his way with the ordinary people, and she too had the gift of talking easily to the merchants, smiths, washerwomen and servant girls who crowded out on to the streets to see her go by. She spoke to them in her native Scots, with no trace of a French accent, laughing and joking and somehow making each one feel like an old friend, although she never lost any of her natural dignity.

She was lively and high-spirited, and one of the things she missed most was the gaiety of the French Court. The Scottish Lords took themselves very seriously. They were so gloomy, she complained, that she found herself longing for joy and laughter. She was full of fun herself, with a quick wit and a sharp tongue. She loved dancing, masques, hunting and pageantry and she drew her courtiers into the half-forgotten pleasures of royal balls and banquets almost against their will. She was always calm and determinedly pleasant with the ones who made obvious their hostility to her, though they suspected that she laughed at them behind their backs. Alone in the evenings with her four Maries, some of her French servants and her nearest Scottish relatives, she would sit and gossip, joking about the behaviour of her subjects, and then she would gamble at cards until the small hours of the morning.

However, even if they felt excluded from her little circle of intimates, none of her nobles could complain that she neglected affairs of state. She relied most upon Lord James and William Maitland of Lethington, the experienced diplomat who had become her secretary, seeking information and advice from them, but she did not allow them to tell her what to do. She was Queen, and no one could command her. She would sit quietly at privy council meetings, stitching away at her needlework, smiling a little to herself as she listened, and then at the end of all the arguments she would put her own views in unmistakable terms, with both honesty and forcefulness. She learned quickly. Soon she had a keen grasp of what was going on around her, and she thoroughly enjoyed the exercise of power.

Her policy of religious toleration was already working well; her agreement to a scheme providing the Reformed Church with revenues and her willingness to allow those who heard Mass to be prosecuted won her many friends and at first she had high hopes of her other main concern, her relationship with England. There is no doubt that she expected friendship from the English Queen for, as she had explained to Elizabeth's ambassador before she left France, 'We are both in one isle, both of one language, both the nearest kinswoman that each other hath, and both Queens.'

With so many interests in common, they could surely reach an understanding. As part of that understanding, Mary desperately wanted

71. Carved wooden cupboard, believed to have been owned by Mary's mother.
(National Museums of Scotland)

to be recognised as Elizabeth's heir, but there lay the great stumbling block to an agreement between them. Elizabeth could not forget that Mary had quartered the English arms with her own, and, however much the Queen of Scots protested that it had not been her own doing, that her father-in-law had forced her into it, the English remained extremely suspicious.

When Maitland of Lethington was sent to London to raise the matter, Elizabeth at once demanded to know whether Mary had now ratified the Treaty of Edinburgh. Maitland conveyed her refusal as tactfully as he could, and it was a tribute to his diplomacy that Elizabeth did not fly into a rage but explained her own viewpoint calmly enough. To ask her to name her successor, she said, was like asking her to place her own winding sheet before her eyes.

Everyone knew that a monarch felt threatened by his heir, because there were always discontented subjects ready to rebel and try to put the heir on the throne instead. If she recognised Mary's rights, she would be as good as inviting the English Catholics to rise up in support of the Queen of

72. *Queen Elizabeth of England* in 1559. (National Portrait Gallery, London)

Scots. She did admit, with some reluctance, that she preferred Mary to any other candidate, but she could not commit herself beyond that point.

Mary was reasonably satisfied when she heard the details of the audience, and she embarked upon a campaign of reassuring Elizabeth about her intentions. Throughout the autumn she wrote her long letters and plied her with gifts, exchanging valuable rings with her as a token of friendship. By the New Year she had even persuaded the English Queen to discuss a personal meeting in York that summer. Mary wanted that above all else, for she felt sure that any possible misunderstandings between them would be banished forever if only they could talk to each other face to face. It therefore came as a cruel blow to her when, in the late spring, Elizabeth cancelled the encounter. Despite all Catherine de Medici's efforts, war had broken out in France between Catholics and Protestants, and Elizabeth felt that she could not afford to hold a public meeting with a half-French, Catholic Queen. If she did, she would antagonise all her Protestant supporters.

When Mary received the news she was bitterly upset. Always easily moved to tears, she wept so much that she had to retire to bed for the rest

73. *Anne Boleyn*, Queen Elizabeth's mother, by an unknown artist. (National Portrait Gallery, London)

of the day. Elizabeth had spoken only of a postponement, not a cancellation, her advisers pointed out, but who knew when the opportunity to speak to each other in person would come again?

After several days of misery and depression, the Queen's fighting spirit reasserted itself. If she could not go south to York, she would undertake another journey instead. She would make a progress through the northern parts of her own kingdom. She had been intending to do so ever since she had arrived and had delayed going only because of her hopes for the southern trip. Urged on by Lord James, she resolved to spend a month in Aberdeen, then travel on to Inverness. Enjoying as she did the encouraging response of the local people wherever she went, she was cheered by the prospect of the journey, although it was not merely a pleasure jaunt.

Lord James was particularly anxious that she should take action against her influential subject, the Earl of Huntly, whose lands were near

74. The Earl of Huntly's bedchamber at Huntly Castle.
(Historic Buildings and Monuments, SDD)

Aberdeen. The Earl should have been Mary's principal Scottish supporter, given his religion and his close relationship with her, for he was a grandson of James IV and so her cousin. He was extremely powerful, living on his estates in near royal style, and in other circumstances he could have been useful as her representative in the north.

Within months of her return, however, there was a coolness between them. The Earl was of an older generation, forty-eight to Mary's nineteen, he had been brought up with James V and he probably felt that she did not pay enough attention to him. That in itself was hardly surprising. He had a long history of underhand dealings with the English, and according to the English ambassador he was so devious that 'no man will trust him either in word or deed'. He was at loggerheads with his other cousin, the Protestant Lord James, and their mutual jealousy and dislike were about to erupt into a much more violent disagreement.

For some years past, there had been no Earl of Moray. That title had last been held by one of James IV's illegitimate sons. It was an honour worth having, for it brought with it valuable lands in the north. These lay close to Huntly territory, and in the absence of any legal owner, the Earl of Huntly had been administering the estates and drawing the revenues. Now, in the winter of 1561–2, the Queen was persuaded to grant the title secretly to Lord James. Sooner or later, Huntly would have to know, because he would be forced to hand over the Moray estates, but he was going to be annoyed, to say the least.

Hoping for a tactful solution, the Queen had kept the grant secret but she was losing patience with Huntly herself. He angered her by arrogantly criticising her religious policies, declaring that she was being far too kind to the Protestants, and there was a tiresome incident when his son, Sir John Gordon, became involved in an unsavoury feud, wounded Lord Ogilvy during a fight on the streets of Edinburgh and later escaped from prison and fled north. The time had come to show the Earl that he and his family could not flout the law.

Travelling with an impressive entourage, Mary made her way through Perthshire and Angus to Aberdeen, where at once she received a visit from Lady Huntly who had come to beg for her son's life. The Queen replied carefully that she could not pardon Sir John unless he returned to prison. This he did, but the confinement proved more than he could bear and before long he escaped again, gathered an army of horsemen and prepared to attack the royal procession as it moved further north. His idea was to seize the Queen and force her to marry him. The fact that he already had a wife did not deter him.

Alarmed and indignant, Mary cancelled her plans to visit his father's stronghold at Strathbogie, and instead she went to the Moray castle of Darnaway. There she announced her gift of the earldom to Lord James and, as she anticipated, Huntly and his family were furious. When she arrived at Inverness, to stay at the royal castle there, its keeper refused to open the gates to her, for he was another of Huntly's sons. That was treason. Even the Earl was dismayed when he heard and he quickly sent a message ordering him to admit the Queen. His son obeyed, whereupon the captain of the castle was promptly seized by Mary's men and hanged from the castle walls.

After this grim beginning, Mary spent a surprisingly happy interlude at Inverness. She imagined that she had done enough to show Huntly that he must submit. She had asserted her authority successfully, she believed, and she was exhilarated by her brush with danger. When the Highland chiefs came to call upon her, she told them she was sorry that she was not a man, for then she could have known what is was to lie all night in the fields, or walk upon the street with a helmet and a sword.

When she set out on the journey back to Aberdeen, though, it became apparent that her troubles were not over. Sir John Gordon and his horsemen reappeared on the horizon, shadowing the royal cavalcade, and there were unmistakable signs that his father was making military preparations. Lord James, now recognised as Earl of Moray, advised the Queen to send for reinforcements, and on 16 October, Huntly and his son were outlawed. At that, Sir John sent Mary the keys of his two castles. She accepted them, commenting drily that she did not need them: she had other ways of opening Gordon doors.

Shortly afterwards, Huntly marched towards Aberdeen, declaring that he would seize Mary and marry her to whomsoever he chose. Until then, neither Mary nor Maitland of Lethington had been altogether convinced of the Earl's villainy, but now there could be no mistake. The Earl of Moray had been right. He and Maitland took the field at the head of the Queen's forces and the two armies met at Corrichie. There, early on the morning of 28 October 1562, Maitland made a stirring speech, urging the royal forces to remember their loyalty to the crown. For his part, Huntly was in two minds about joining in the combat until the very last moment. Stout and unfit, he was in terror of his life but in the end he decided that he would have to fight and, dropping to his knees, he began to pray.

'O Lord!' he cried, 'I have been a bloodthirsty man, and by my means has much innocent blood been spilt. But wilt Thou give me victory this day, and I shall serve Thee all the days of my life!'

The battle which followed was swift and decisive. Moray and Maitland fell upon the rebels and routed them completely. Huntly was captured, and, when it was all over, he was placed upon his horse and led before the royal generals. At that very moment he suffered a sudden stoke and he fell from his horse, dead. His body was taken by sea to Edinburgh, embalmed, and finally brought to trial before the Queen and her parliament. In a macabre scene, his coffin was placed upon end 'as if the Earl stood upon his feet' and his corpse was solemnly convicted of treason, condemned and forfeited. His son, Sir John, had also been captured at Corrichie. He was tried and condemned to death. The Queen was forced to witness his execution, for her advisers said that if she were not there people would believe that she had encouraged Sir John in his scheme to marry her. When the executioner bungled his work she was distraught, and she had to be carried to her chamber, weeping hysterically.

4
THE SUITORS

IN THE autumn months after Corrichie, when news of Huntly's downfall had ceased to be a sensation, people turned once more to an old and favourite topic of conversation. As John Knox put it, 'The marriage of our Queen was in all men's mouths.' Who would Mary marry? She had been a widow for a year now and it was time she thought seriously about taking another husband.

No one was more aware of the problem than Mary herself and, as always, she knew exactly what she wanted to do. She wanted to marry Don Carlos and, in spite of all Catherine de Medici's efforts the previous year, Philip II was showing distinct signs of interest again. He seemed not only willing but positively eager to go along with the idea, and he gave Mary to understand that, if she were his daughter-in-law, he would lose no time in raising Catholic support in England so that he could depose Elizabeth and put Mary on the throne instead.

Mary did not see the situation in quite those terms. She was more concerned with securing her own position in Scotland and she knew that a powerful ally was what she needed. Moreover, she had no intention of abandoning her own kingdom. Philip II had already shown the way.

75. Drawing of Mary about 1561 from the Forman Armorial, expressing the wish that 'the Lord be ever her Protector, and make her marriage as he thinks best, that her lieges may . . . in peace rest'. (National Library of Scotland)

76. *Philip II, King of Spain,* father of Don Carlos, by an unknown artist. (National Portrait Gallery, London)

When he married Mary Tudor he visited England from time to time, but Mary Tudor remained in her own country, ruling it for herself with his backing. That was exactly the situation Mary, Queen of Scots wanted to repeat. She would stay in Scotland, ruling the country personally. Don Carlos was welcome to live with her until he inherited the throne of Spain but what she wanted from the match was not a loving husband but an influential friend.

Surprisingly, her preference for Don Carlos was supported by a significant number of her Protestant Lords, some of whom were willing to favour any alliance as long as it was not with France. With their support, the Queen went ahead determinedly with her negotiations and throughout 1563 she seemed to place more and more reliance on the Spanish marriage providing the answer to all her problems.

This was understandable enough, for that year was to bring her a series of personal crises which plunged her into despair for weeks at a time. The first of these was the tragic affair of Pierre de Châtelard, the poet, an aristocratic young man who was a member of her household. Gallant, accomplished and pleasing in his ways, he was exactly the sort of companion who helped to beguile her when she was homesick for France. He composed poems for her and flirted with her lightheartedly, but he never passed the bounds of accepted etiquette.

77. *Don Carlos*, by Sanchez Coello, who painted it for his father and therefore flattered the young man's appearance.
(The Prado, Madrid)

All was well until one night when she was staying at Rossend Castle, near Burntisland in Fife. Carried away with love and admiration for her, he hid himself beneath the voluminous draperies of her bed. When he was discovered there by the grooms of her chamber, who checked her apartment every evening, he excused himself by saying that, as the Queen sat up late discussing business with Moray and Maitland, he had been overcome by tiredness. Longing for a quiet place to sleep, he had unthinkingly found it in the royal bedchamber next door.

When the Queen was told about his escapade the following morning she was affronted by his insolence and she banished him from her Court. Infatuated with her to the point of suicidal recklessness, Châtelard ignored her orders and followed her to St Andrews. There he forced his way into her chamber while her ladies helped her prepare for bed. This time he could not be forgiven. His behaviour had amounted to lèse majesté and posed a serious threat to her security. He was seized, imprisoned in St Andrews Castle, tried publicly and sentenced to death. On 22 February he was executed in the market square. As he stood on the scaffold, he recited the poet Ronsard's 'Hymn to Death' and then he turned in the direction of the house where the Queen was staying.

'Adieu, the most beautiful and the most cruel princess in the world!' he exclaimed, and those were the last words he spoke.

Châtelard's death was the first in a series. Just two days later, Mary's uncle, the Duke of Guise, was assassinated, shot in the back by a French Protestant. When she heard the news her tears flowed 'like showers of rain', it was said. A few weeks after that, another Guise uncle died and later on she lost one of her Stewart half-brothers. Miserably, she remarked that God always took from her those persons in whom she had the greatest pleasure, nor were her spirits improved by growing opposition to her Spanish plans.

At the end of May, John Knox got wind of the marriage scheme and he preached furiously against it from his pulpit. Mary, wretched and upset by her recent bereavements, took his behaviour more to heart than she had ever done before. Once more she summoned him to her presence and, according to his description, when he and his companion John Erskine of Dun were shown into her cabinet, she was already in a 'vehement fume'. As soon as she saw him she exclaimed that never was a monarch treated by anyone as she was by him.

'I have borne with you in all your rigorous manner of speaking,' she cried, 'both against myself and against my uncles, yea I have sought your favours by all possible means. I offered unto you presence and audience whensoever it pleased you to admonish me and yet I cannot be quit of you! I avow to God I shall be once revenged!'

With that she burst into tears, sobbing so violently that Marnac, her little page boy, ran to fetch her another handkerchief and even Knox felt uncomfortable. He had only been pointing out the error of her ways, he muttered.

'But what have ye to do with my marriage?' she demanded indignantly, 'Or what are ye within this commonwealth?'

'A subject born within the same,' he replied self-righteously, and she was reduced to tears again. Erskine of Dun, a more gentle character, tried to calm her and Knox told her,

'I never delighted in the weeping of any of God's creatures, yea I can scarcely well abide the tears of my own boys whom my own hand corrects, much less can I rejoice in Your Majesty's weeping.'

Mary, furious and upset, would not forget the interview. Some months later, she summoned Knox before the Council for involvement in a further disturbance, and, when she entered the chamber, she infuriated him by laughing and saying to her friends,

'Yon man made me greet [cry], and grat never a tear himself. I will see if I can make him greet!' That was not so easily accomplished, however.

Knox was not the only person to be disturbed by the thought of the Spanish marriage. The last thing Queen Elizabeth wanted was for the Queen of Scots to marry a powerful Catholic ally and she was determined to deflect her from her purpose. She let it be known that, if Mary married an Englishman of whom she approved, she might just consider nominating her as her heir.

It was a bait the Queen of Scots could not resist, although the first candidate Elizabeth offered was not one she would have chosen for

78. Pearl necklace reputed to have belonged to Mary. (Reproduced by permission of His Grace the Duke of Norfolk and the Baroness Herries)

79. *William Cecil, Lord Burghley,* Queen Elizabeth's chief adviser, painted about 1560–70 and attributed to Bronckorst. (National Portrait Gallery, London)

80. *Robert Dudley, Earl of Leicester,* Queen Elizabeth's favourite: a miniature by Nicholas Hilliard, 1576. (National Portrait Gallery, London)

herself. Even that experienced diplomat Maitland of Lethington, was disconcerted when Elizabeth offered a man 'in whom', she said, 'nature has implanted so many graces that if she wished to marry she would prefer him to all the princes in the world'. That man was Lord Robert Dudley.

To say that Maitland was startled is an understatement. Dudley was the last person anyone would have expected Elizabeth to select, for a variety of reasons. It was true that he was dark and handsome, but his father had been executed for treason. His first wife, Amy Robsart, had been found dead in very suspicious circumstances. Worst of all, everyone believed Dudley to be Queen Elizabeth's lover. Some thought that if she married anyone it would be him. Others believed that they were already man and wife.

Maitland, always the diplomat, told Elizabeth smoothly that 'this was a great proof of the love she bore to his Queen, that she was willing to give her a thing so dearly prized by herself'. However, he thought that, even if Mary loved Lord Robert as dearly as Elizabeth did, she would not marry him and so deprive the English Queen of 'all the joy and solace she receiveth from his companionship'.

Elizabeth, who always enjoyed a bout of verbal fencing, replied merrily that it was a pity Lord Robert's brother did not have his grace and good looks, for then she and Mary could have had a Dudley each. The subject was turned aside as a joke, but the late summer brought a new

81. Imaginary drawing of Mary, from a petition sent to her in 1565 from the Scots College in Paris: from the Book of Grisy. (Scottish Catholic Archives)

development that changed the situation dramatically. On 6 August 1564, Philip II announced that the Spanish marriage could not take place after all. His negotiations with the Scots were at an end. For a variety of diplomatic reasons he had reached the conclusion that the Scottish alliance would be more trouble than it was worth, and in any case it had become painfully obvious that Don Carlos was in no fit state to marry anyone. In pursuit, so it was said, of a serving woman, the unfortunate youth had fallen headlong downstairs, and for weeks he lay paralysed and blind. A daring operation to remove a piece of his skull relieved the pressure on his brain and gave him back his sight and his power of movement, but he was left subject to alarming fits of homicidal mania. He could not be allowed to marry any woman, least of all the monarch of another country.

Mary was devastated by Philip's decision. She had been so sure that this time the scheme would go through, and that, in spite of her difficulties, the

82. Book belonging to Mary, Queen of Scots: *Chronicle of Savoy*, published in Lyons in 1552 and bound in leather with Mary's royal arms of Scotland.
(The Earl of Rosebery)

promise of Spanish support would transform her life in Scotland. The shattering of her hopes was a terrible blow, and, when she did finally accept that she would never be the wife of Don Carlos, the suggested match with Lord Robert Dudley assumed a whole new significance.

It did for Elizabeth too, of course. She was vastly relieved that Philip would not become Mary's father-in-law, but she did not want her turning her attention to some other Catholic Prince. She was anxious that the Queen of Scots should remain single and the best way of achieving that was to present her with several possible candidates who would keep her occupied for months if not years. Of course if Mary showed signs of actually marrying any of them, she would step in and veto the betrothal. The suitors, being her own subjects, would have to obey her. In pursuance of this complicated policy, she began by making Lord Robert Dudley more attractive by creating him Earl of Leicester. At the same time, she introduced another suitor whom Mary could not ignore: Henry, Lord Darnley.

Darnley was the son of two important people. His father, the Earl of

83. *Henry, Lord Darnley*, at the age of ten, by Hans Eworth, 1555.
(Scottish National Portrait Gallery)

Lennox, was one of Scotland's leading noblemen. Lennox was descended from a Stewart Princess and he claimed that he and not the head of the house of Hamilton was heir to the Scottish throne. His enemies had managed to have him banished from Scotland twenty years before. He had thereupon settled in England with his wife, Lady Margaret Douglas.

Lady Margaret had an equally interesting inheritance, for her mother was the sister of Henry VIII and in fact, after Mary, she was Elizabeth's next heir. She was a devout Catholic and Roman Catholics in England looked to her for leadership. She had two sons, the elder of whom was Lord Darnley. Because of his Tudor relationship, his ambitious mother saw him as a possible King of England and therefore she had him educated carefully and trained in all the courtly accomplishments. Like his father, he was a fine sportsman and he grew into a tall, fair-haired, pretty youth who was utterly spoiled by his doting parents. Nothing was too good for him and only the most elevated lady could be suitable as his wife.

When Francis II was crowned at Rheims, Lady Lennox sent her son to France with a request that Lennox should be restored to his Scottish estates. He met his cousin Mary, Queen of Scots on that occasion and when Francis died he was back again to offer his family's condolences. Already, his mother imagined a marvellous future for him. He should marry the widowed Queen of Scots. Of course, she could do nothing which would draw Elizabeth's attention to her ambition, but now Elizabeth's own machinations led her to use Darnley as the latest pawn in her dealings with Mary.

She first drew the Scots' attention to him at the ceremony where she granted Dudley his peerage. The Scottish emissary, Sir James Melville, was at Westminster for the occasion and he described the scene that day. Lord Robert, he wrote, 'keeping a great gravity and discreet behaviour,' knelt before Elizabeth but she was not quite so dignified. In fact, she 'could not refrain from putting her hand in his neck to tickle him smilingly, the French ambassador and I standing by'. This conduct might hardly suit the occasion, but Elizabeth was obviously in one of her playful moods. Turning to Sir James, she asked him how he liked the new Earl of Leicester. He framed a polite reply, whereupon she remarked archly, 'Yet you like better of yonder long lad,' and she pointed across the chamber to the tall youth who had carried the sword of honor before her when she entered the appartment for the ceremony. It was Lord Darnley. 'No woman of spirit would make choice of such a man that was more like a woman than a man,' replied Sir James tartly, 'for he was very lusty, beardless and lady-faced'. He then changed the subject and Elizabeth let the matter drop.

For the next few days she seemed much more interested in eliciting information about Mary herself. What did the Queen of Scots look like? What colour was her hair? 'Which of them two was fairest?' an embarrassing question to which Sir James replied guardedly that she was the fairest Queen in England 'and ours the fairest Queen in Scotland'. She wanted to know who was the taller. On hearing that it was Mary, she replied, 'Then she is too high' and announced smugly that she herself was 'neither too high nor too low'. When he mentioned that Mary played the

84. *Margaret, Countess of Lennox*, mother of Lord Darnley, by an unknown artist.
(Reproduced by gracious permission of Her Majesty The Queen)

85. Gold pomander believed to have belonged to Mary.
(Reproduced by gracious permission of Her Majesty The Queen)

MARY'S ENGLISH RELATIVES

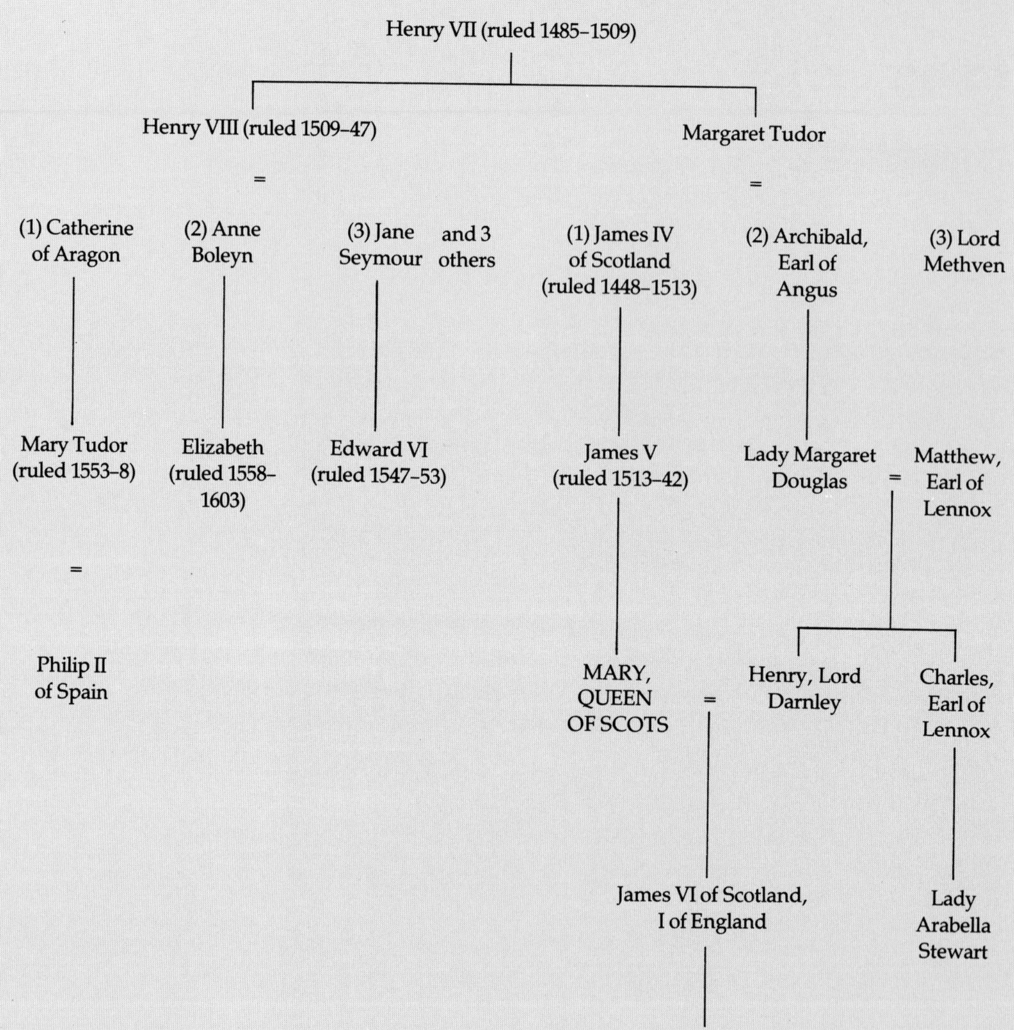

Henry VII (ruled 1485–1509)

- Henry VIII (ruled 1509–47) =
  - (1) Catherine of Aragon
    - Mary Tudor (ruled 1553–8) = Philip II of Spain
  - (2) Anne Boleyn
    - Elizabeth (ruled 1558–1603)
  - (3) Jane Seymour
    - Edward VI (ruled 1547–53)
  - and 3 others
- Margaret Tudor =
  - (1) James IV of Scotland (ruled 1448–1513)
    - James V (ruled 1513–42)
      - MARY, QUEEN OF SCOTS = Henry, Lord Darnley
        - James VI of Scotland, I of England
  - (2) Archibald, Earl of Angus
    - Lady Margaret Douglas = Matthew, Earl of Lennox
      - Henry, Lord Darnley
      - Charles, Earl of Lennox
        - Lady Arabella Stewart
  - (3) Lord Methven

86. Miniature of Mary, placing a wedding ring on her finger: the ring was worn on the right hand: by an unknown artist. (Reproduced by gracious permission of Her Majesty The Queen)

lute and the virginals, Elizabeth so arranged matters that whenever he came upon her she was either playing an instrument, dancing, or displaying some other talent. The more she learned about Mary, the more did she become convinced that Darnley was the ideal person to take up her attention, and that September she set her plan in motion by giving the Earl of Lennox permission to go to Scotland.

Not everyone was pleased to see him back, but Mary welcomed him and restored him to his extensive estates in the west of Scotland. Almost at once the rumours started. Would his son follow him, and if so, would he woo and marry the Queen of Scots? Mary spent Christmas that year in Edinburgh, and about the middle of January she moved over to Fife.

87. Wemyss Castle, where Mary met Darnley again. (Photograph, Michael Brooks)

On 10 February Lord Darnley crossed the Border into Scotland. He was going to Court and on 16 February he reached Wemyss Castle. The following day, he and Mary met for the third time in their lives.

The Queen greeted the new arrival with interest, for she was aware of his significance. She welcomed him as a cousin, since they were both grandchildren of Margaret Tudor, and she seemed favourably impressed with him. Sir James Melville, who was there, remembered afterwards that she 'took well with him, and said that he was the lustiest and best-proportioned long man that she had seen, for he was of high stature, long and small (that is, finely built), even and erect, from his youth well instructed in all honest and comely exercises'.

Carefully trained by his mother, Darnley assumed with Mary a courteous, deferential manner which went down well with her, all the more so since some of her Lords paid scant attention to such niceties of behaviour. There is no evidence, though, that she fell instantly in love with him. Her mind was on other matters. She was sending messages south with assurances that she would do all she could to please Elizabeth, and now that Don Carlos had been removed from the scene she was inclined to accept Leicester as a husband. She believed that Elizabeth was sincere in her promises to recognise her as her heir if she married in accordance with her wishes. Mary's advisers had misgivings, but, as usual, she was determined to have her own way.

The initial encounter with Darnley at Wemyss Castle was brief. Having been presented, he left for Dunkeld to pay his respects to his father. However, encouraged by his welcome at Court and eager to pursue his mission, he was back again by the end of the week, ready to cross the Forth with the royal cavalcade at North Queensferry and ride back to Edinburgh with them.

From then onwards he was a constant member of Mary's entourage. He fitted in very well with the other members of her circle, the ladies, the courtiers and the foreign attendants who had, like her, been abroad and knew the ways of other countries. Darnley soon struck up a particular friendship with her Italian secretary, David Riccio, and together they provided the kind of relaxing company that she always enjoyed. She danced the galliard with Darnley, invited him to join her at cards in the evening and was pleased to find that he shared her love of hunting. In short, he was a welcome addition to her household, but nothing more: nothing more, that is, until Queen Elizabeth suddenly announced that even if Mary did marry Leicester, she could not be recognised as her heir.

Mary took the news badly. She realised now that what she had long suspected was true. Elizabeth was simply amusing herself at her expense. The Leicester marriage had been nothing more than a ploy, an empty promise to win time. She had made a fool of Mary and although the Queen of Scots strove to hide her feelings from Elizabeth's messenger, he learned that once he had gone she 'wept her fill'.

Angry and disillusioned, she vowed that she would no longer try to please anyone. She would rely on her own judgment and marry whom she chose. Lady Lennox was constantly urging her to select Lord Darnley, promising that he would be respectful and would treat her well. He was an agreeable companion and although he was only nineteen his very youth appealed to her. Accustomed as she was to taking the leader's part, she saw in him someone she could mould, train up to be the consort she needed. She would teach him to understand the political and religious situation in Scotland and he would lend her actions the masculine authority that her turbulent nobles seemed to need. Best of all, he would be hers alone. He would be utterly loyal to her, for he would owe her everything. He was not a prince, of course, but the blood of both the Stewart and the Tudor royal families flowed in his veins. Elizabeth would not dare to utter a word of criticism, since it was she who had sent him north in the first place.

In several of these calculations Mary was dreadfully wrong, not least in her assumption that Elizabeth would approve. Nothing was further from the English Queen's intentions than that the Queen of Scots should marry the young man seen by many as a claimant to her own throne. Mary's Lords were outraged too. The Earl of Moray was particularly jealous, horrified at the thought that he was to be ousted as her principal adviser by an ignorant, arrogant youth. Indeed, the hostility of all the nobles was so evident that the English ambassador remarked,

'What shall become of him I know not, but it is greatly to be feared that

88. Stirling Castle, a general view. (Historic Buildings and Monuments, SDD)

89. Stirling Castle, the Palace block built by Mary's father. (Historic Buildings and Monuments, SDD)

he can have no long life amongst this people.'

The ambassador could see that Mary was doing all she could to transform Darnley into a fitting consort, and he went on, 'The Queen herself, being of better understanding, seeketh to frame and fashion him to the nature of her subjects', but it was to no purpose, for 'no persuasion can alter that which custom hath made old in him. He is counted proud, disdainful and suspicious. A greater plague to her [Mary] there cannot be, a greater benefit to the Queen's Majesty [Elizabeth] could not have chanced.'

That spring, Mary disagreed with almost all her usual advisers, even quarrelling with the four Maries, and the more opposition she encountered the more determined did she become that she would please herself in this regardless of the opinions of others.

In her determination she deliberately closed her eyes to the less pleasing aspects of Darnley's character and, as chance would have it, she had less opportunity than might otherwise have been expected to assess his true worth. In early April he fell ill, and after a day or two spent trying to shake off what he took to be a cold, it became obvious that he had caught measles. He was staying at Stirling Castle at the time and the Queen became a frequent visitor to his chamber. Revelling in her attention, Darnley was all sweetness and pathetic gratitude. When his natural peevishness did come to the surface it was easy to blame it on his tiresome illness. Mary was sorry for him. Her long experience of nursing Francis through his various ailments had taught her how to cherish and divert an invalid and she spent a good deal of time at his bedside, looking in upon him late at night as well as throughout the day.

Needless to say, gossip spread like wildfire and the malicious

90. Stirling Castle, inside the kitchens.
(Historic Buildings and Monuments, SDD)

91. Stone fireplace in the royal apartments at Stirling Castle.
(Historic Buildings and Monuments, SDD)

92. Decorative wooden roundel from ceiling at Stirling Castle, showing a jester.
(Historic Buildings and Monuments, SDD)

whispering of the courtiers had the effect of making the Queen feel all the more protective of him. She began to behave with a defiant recklessness, deliberately flaunting her affection for him. It was not that she had fallen madly in love with him: rather, she was using him for her own purposes and the strain of trying to convince herself that she was doing the right thing began to tell. Observers noticed a change in her appearance and one visitor even remarked that 'her majesty was laid aside, her wits not such as they were, her beauty other than it was.' It was even said that someone must have cast an evil spell on her and people were quick to blame the fact that one of her few confidantes was now the sinister Lord Ruthven, a man reputed to be a sorcerer.

The situation was not improved when Sir Nicholas Throckmorton, Elizabeth's ambassador, arrived to say that Elizabeth was completely opposed to the match. Mary could choose any other noble in England, but she would be recognised as heir only if she selected the Earl of Leicester. The Queen of Scots was furious at what she took to be another cynical example of Elizabeth's insincerity. She told Throckmorton coldly that she would wait three months until she married so that Elizabeth would have time to send her approval, but she was most certainly not going to change her mind. The very same day she created Darnley Earl of Ross, which amounted to announcing their engagement.

Elizabeth flew into a fury when she heard and on 2 July she sent an imperious order north, recalling both Lennox and his son to England. Mary, already overwrought, burst into tears when the message came, but she was not to be browbeaten. She refused to let them go. By now she had persuaded Philip II of Spain to give his approval to the match, Charles IX had similarly agreed to it and her uncle, the Cardinal of Lorraine, referred irritatedly to his niece's fiancé as 'a girlish nincompoop' but nevertheless set about getting the papal dispensation needed to allow her to marry her cousin.

1563

By mid-July it was obvious that the wedding was imminent even though the three-month period Mary had promised Elizabeth was not yet up. On 16 July, Mary and Darnley rode to Seton Palace, home of her faithful supporter Lord Seton, and they spent two nights there, giving rise to all manner of unsavoury rumours. Back in Edinburgh they dined at the Castle and then in the afternoon Mary diguised herself in men's costume and they wandered about the town together. 'This manner of passing to and fro,' said the English ambassador, 'gave again occasion to many men to muse what might be her meaning', and with every day that passed the courtiers found Darnley more and more intolerable. As one of them said, 'His words to all men against whom he conceiveth any displeasure, how unjust soever it be, are so proud and spiteful that rather he seemeth a monarch of the world than he that not long since we have seen and known, the Lord Darnley.'

On Sunday, 22 July, the banns for the marriage were called and the Queen created her fiancé Duke of Albany. The following Saturday she announced that, when she married Prince Henry, he would be styled King of Scots. It was not legally within her powers to grant him that title, for the decision had to be taken in parliament, but she ignored that. She was Queen of Scots and so her husband must be King simply because she chose to marry him. Needless to say, her Lords were even more angry when this announcement was made.

93. *Lord Darnley and his younger brother, Charles,* painted for their mother by Hans Eworth in 1563 when Darnley was seventeen. (Reproduced by gracious permission of Her Majesty The Queen)

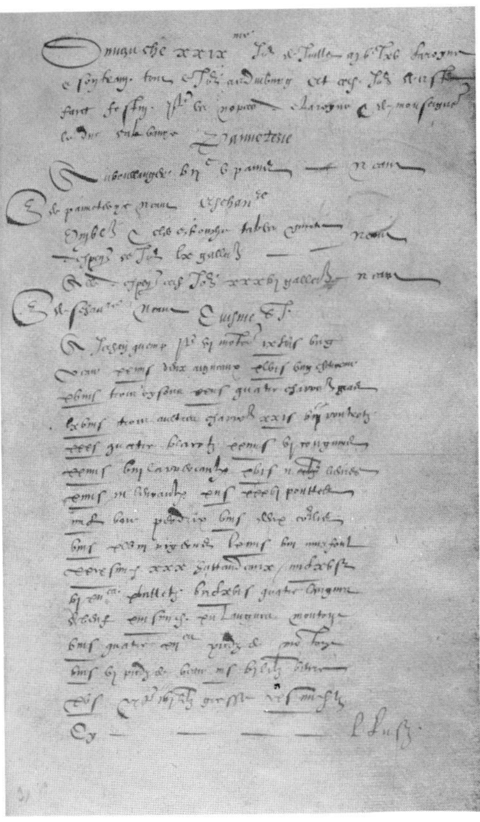

94. Household expenses on the day of Mary's wedding to Darnley: chicken, lamb, game and other provisions listed in French.
(Scottish Record Office)

A week later, on 29 July 1565, they were married. The service took place at six o'clock in the morning in the Queen's private chapel at Holyrood, for it was a Catholic ceremony. The Earl of Lennox and the Earl of Atholl solemnly escorted Mary from her appartments. For her first wedding in Notre Dame she had worn white. Now, because she was a widow, she appeared in deepest mourning, in a black dress and a widow's black hood. It was an outfit very similar to the one she had worn on the day of her first husband's funeral and it symbolised the old life she was leaving behind.

Having led her in procession to the chapel, Lennox and Atholl went away to fetch the bridegroom and the ceremony began. Darnley placed three rings upon the Queen's finger, the middle one set with a splendid diamond. Together, they knelt before the priest and prayers were said. Because Darnley claimed to be a Protestant, he did not wait for the rest of the service. Kissing his bride, he retired to her chamber while she heard Mass.

After that, she followed him to her apartments and the rejoicings began. Her ladies came up to her and began to help her out of her black gown. At first she put on a token show of reluctance, as etiquette demanded, then she allowed everyone present to remove a pin from her garments. The widow's weeds were taken away and instead her ladies attired her in a magnificent new kirtle and gown in bright colours.

The Queen and her husband rested until midday, then, to the sounding of trumpets, they walked in procession to the hall, where a sumptuous banquet awaited them. As a sign of good fortune, handfuls of coins were thrown to the bystanders 'in great abundance', and later there was dancing. That evening, an equally lavish supper was held, followed by more dancing, 'and so they go to bed'.

5

HENRY, KING OF SCOTS

THE DAY after the wedding, the Queen gathered her Lords together for a solemn ceremony. The heralds proclaimed Darnley to be King of Scots, and they announced that in future all official documents would be issued by 'both their Majesties, as King and Queen of Scotland, conjointly'. This announcement ought to have been greeted by a rousing cheer, but instead there was an ominous silence. At last, one lone voice was heard. The new King's father, the Earl of Lennox, proudly shouted out, 'God save His Grace', but no one else spoke.

The Lords were, of course, furious that Mary had granted her husband the title without their consent, but at least she had not given him the crown matrimonial for life. That would have meant that not only would he rule Scotland along with her, but also if anything happened to her, he would continue as King of Scots, and, if he married again and had a son, the child would one day inherit the crown. Mary had decided that he was not yet ready for such a responsibility. All the same, there was fierce resentment of him. Obviously, none of the Hamiltons was going to approve of a Lennox being raised to such high rank, and Darnley's own behaviour had

95. Silver medal commemorating the marriage of Mary and Darnley, dated 1565. (Scottish National Portrait Gallery)

96. 1565 coin marked 'Mary and Henry, by the grace of God Queen and King of Scots' (in Latin), with a design of a tortoise climbing a palm tree on the other side. (National Museums of Scotland)

antagonised almost everyone else, beginning with the Earl of Moray.

From the very first, the two had resented each other and a mere five weeks after Darnley's arrival in Scotland he managed to make the situation much worse. Another of the Queen's half-brothers, Lord Robert Stewart, had been showing the young man a map of Scotland and he pointed out where Moray's extensive lands lay. At this, 'the Lord Darnley said that it was too much'. Possibly through Lord Robert himself, Moray got to hear of the remark and he hurried off at once to complain to Mary. She ordered her protégé to apologise, but even if he obeyed her the damage was done, and from that time onwards the ill-feeling between the two increased and involved the Queen as well.

By the time of the marriage, such was the distrust between them that Moray claimed that Darnley was plotting to murder him, and Mary heard alarming rumours that Moray planned to kidnap Darnley and Lennox and send them forcibly back to England. When Moray repeatedly ignored Mary's orders to appear before her, she decided that she could stand no more of his defiance and on 6 August she had him denounced as an outlaw. Almost three years before, he and she had ridden north against her overmighty vassal the Earl of Huntly. Now she prepared to take the field against Moray himself.

Declaring that she would rather lose her crown altogether than fail to be revenged on him for his disloyalty, she raised an army and rode out against him, Darnley at her side, a glittering figure in his gilded armour. Moray and his friends had been in the west. They now rode to Edinburgh, hoping for reinforcements, and the Queen was relentless in her pursuit of them. She had moved across Scotland, hoping to encounter them. Now she went back towards the capital, riding undaunted through pouring rain and earning the admiration even of John Knox. He noted that although 'the most part waxed weary, the Queen's courage increased, man-like, so much that she was ever with the foremost'.

Disappointed at the response in Edinburgh, Moray now pinned his hopes on help from Queen Elizabeth and he moved south towards Dumfries. When no help came, he and his friends slipped across the Border. Still in a mood of vengeful determination, wearing a pistol at her belt, the Queen arrived there to find him gone. The Earl of Bothwell had recently returned from exile, and she had made him her Lieutenant-General, so she left him in the south-west and she herself rode for Edinburgh once more. The aptly named 'Chaseabout Raid' was over. Meanwhile, Moray and his companions rode to London, obtained an audience with Queen Elizabeth and begged for her help. She told them curtly that they had rebelled against their rightful monarch and that they were lucky that she did not put them in prison. Had their rebellion succeeded, it would have been different, but she wanted no part of their failure.

Back in Edinburgh, Mary, Queen of Scots could now turn her attention to ruling the country with a husband by her side. The first weeks of their married life had scarcely been as she had envisaged, but now she could settle down to the serious business of training King Henry to share her duties. After only a few weeks, however, she began to recognise with

97. The Scottish crown, remodelled for Mary's father in 1540.

deep dismay that he was not living up to her expectations. Even in the middle of their military preparations, they had quarrelled violently over who should be Lieutenant-General of the army, for Darnley wanted that position to go to his father and he was peevish and sullen when she chose Bothwell instead.

Riding by her side in his fine armour he had been an agreeable enough companion, but as soon as she became involved once more with the cares of government he was bored and he fancied that she neglected him. Instead of reading state papers with her, he went off hunting. This was very awkward because now that documents had to go out under his name

98. The Scottish sceptre, given to Mary's grandfather by the Pope.

99. The Scottish sword of state, presented to Mary's grandfather.

100. Painted royal Scottish arms from Edinburgh Castle.
(Historic Buildings and Monuments, SDD)

as well as hers, his signature was required before they could be sent. By the late autumn he was so often absent that business was held up and in the end Mary was forced to solve the problem by having a stamp of his signature made so that his name could go on papers even in his absence.

He failed to attend meetings which required his presence, and his attitude to the delicate question of religion was even more exasperating. He had made much of his Protestant sympathies and he had gone to great lengths to avoid being thought a Catholic like his mother. Mary hoped that under her influence he would revert to being a good Catholic, but she needed him to display moderation, as she was doing. In the aftermath of Moray's rebellion, people were more anxious than ever that she might be about to persecute the Protestants, for word had got out that she had written to Philip II of Spain asking for help against her rebels. Now, she wanted to reassure her subjects. She even spoke of hearing Protestant preachers in public herself, and she encouraged Darnley to go and listen to John Knox's sermons. Unfortunately, as an exercise in tact that proved a disaster. Instead of calming general fears by listening appreciatively, her husband took obvious umbrage at some of the minister's remarks which he thought were criticisms of himself. As soon as the service was over, he flung away petulantly, declaring that the sermon had gone on too long, and when he got back to the palace he refused to eat his dinner. In short, he was behaving like a spoiled child.

In other circumstances his behaviour might have been tolerated, passed off as amusing, but by having such a man at her side Mary was placing a dangerous weapon in the hands of her enemies. Those who hated her would sooner or later plot to use him against her, and in the meantime she had to put up with his boorishness. It must have been a source of bitterness to her as well as of consolation when she discovered that she was pregnant.

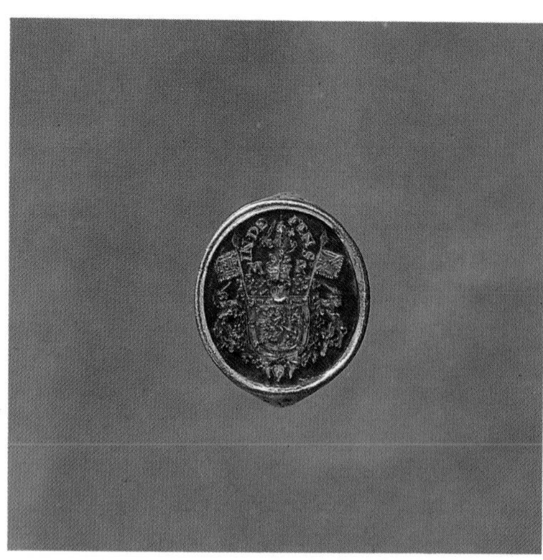

101. Mary's signet ring with her coat of arms. (The Trustees of the British Museum)

The baby had been conceived about the time of her expedition to Dumfries during the 'Chaseabout Raid'. Certainly, by the end of October there were rumours among her friends that she was expecting a child. The following month she was ill, perhaps suffering a nervous reaction after all the excitement of the military expedition, and that rather silenced rumours about her condition, especially when, at the beginning of December, she marked her recovery by throwing herself into a vigorous round of activity, taking as much exercise as she possibly could. The gossips decided that she would never act so rashly if she really were with child, and so it came as a surprise when she chose to travel to Linlithgow by litter instead of on horseback. That was a sure sign. After that, her pregnancy was public knowledge.

News of the disagreements between her husband and herself was also becoming widespread. Darnley was spending an increasing amount of time roaming around the town at night with idle young companions and it was generally said that they went in pursuit of women. He was certainly too fond of drink, and on at least one occasion he reduced the Queen to tears in public by his uncouth behaviour when he had taken too much wine. 'The Lord Darnley followeth his pastimes more than the Queen is content withall', remarked an English observer, and she was soon to give very obvious evidence of her annoyance with him.

A new silver coin was to be issued, commemorating their marriage and its design incorporated the heads of Mary and Darnley in profile, with the words 'Whom God has joined together let no man put asunder', in Latin. When it appeared, it was withdrawn again with startling rapidity, seemingly because it put his name first: it read, 'Henry and Mary, by the Grace of God, King and Queen of Scots'.

This was exactly what most of the official documents did, but Mary had become distinctly sensitive about her husband's claims to power and she was resolutely refusing to grant him the crown matrimonial. It was not for want of pleading and complaining on his part. He was constantly trying to wheedle or browbeat her into agreeing and he was loud in his tales of her

102. Sixteenth-century painted ceiling at Huntingtower, one of the castles visited by Mary. (Historic Buildings and Monuments, SDD)

unsympathetic attitude. Needless to say, there were plenty of Mary's enemies on hand, ready to fan the flames of his anger. They told him that she had no right to put herself first. They said that for all she was a Queen she was still his wife, and everyone knew that a wife took second place to her husband. It was a highly dubious argument but it was what he wanted to hear, and it was not long before his self-appointed friends were telling him that she was not only excluding him from the government of the country but she was being unfaithful to him as well. They alleged that she had taken a lover and, with his vanity and his jealous nature, he was all too easily convinced that their lies were true.

The nobles themselves were feeling neglected, hence their desire to stir up any possible source of trouble for Mary. Moray and Maitland had gone from her counsels, both of them disgusted by her marriage. Darnley himself was totally unfitted to give her any advice, nor was his father much better. She was now consulting increasingly with Lord Home and the Earl of Bothwell, but she also relied upon lesser men of her own household, in particular upon the secretary who dealt with her French correspondence, David Riccio.

Riccio was an Italian, a dark, swarthy man of uncertain age, with deformed shoulders and unpleasing features. People always described him as being hideously ugly, but he made up for that by his cleverness, his quick wit and his ability to amuse. He was also an accomplished musician, and it was this talent which had first brought him to the Queen's notice.

103. Highland harp said to have belonged to Mary. (National Museums of Scotland)

He came to Scotland with the Savoyard ambassador and he was constantly in and about the Court. Mary was passionately fond of music and she employed a group of singers to entertain her. There were three of them, who sang part music and were known as chamber valets. They needed a bass to complete their quartet and Riccio offered his services. The outcome was that, when the Savoyard ambassador returned to Italy, he remained behind and was made a fourth valet of the Queen's chamber.

Possibly any other singer would have stayed in that post for the rest of his career, a minor if necessary member of the retinue. David, however, possessed a driving ambition and he was not content to be a musician all

104. Sixteenth-century Scottish jewel made with a French cameo of Mary: probably a gift by her to one of her supporters. (National Museums of Scotland)

his days. Gradually he insinuated himself into Mary's favour. Not only did she enjoy his music; she laughed at his quips and when, three years later, she had to find a new secretary, she chose him.

He proved to be efficient, and he was also ready to make the most of the opportunity. Compensated at last for his low stature and his unprepossessing features, he strutted about in magnificent silks and velvets, boasting of his influence with the Queen. Soon the Lords found that they were forced to go through him whenever they wanted to approach her with a request, and he made it clear that he was willing to be obliging in return for handsome bribes.

This behaviour earned him their hatred, for they regarded themselves as being the monarch's traditional advisers. Proud of their ancient lineage, they had no intention of humbling themselves before a mere foreign clerk. Sir James Melville remembered long afterwards how 'some of the nobility would gloom upon him and some of them would shoulder him and push him aside when they entered the chamber and found him always speaking with Her Majesty'. Fearing their hostility he had at first courted Darnley's friendship, flattering him and making much of him so that in the early weeks of the marriage it was said that 'David is he that now works all, chief secretary to the Queen and governor to her good man'. Mary saw what was happening. She urged Melville to be kind to 'Seigneur David' who, she said, was 'hated without cause', but it was already too late for her to halt the ill-feeling against him.

Not only did he seem to the nobles to form a barrier between the Queen

105. Painted wooden panel of the Virgin and Child from a house on Castle Hill, Edinburgh, reputed to have belonged to Mary's mother. (National Museums of Scotland)

and themselves, but, because he was a member of her inner household, he had access to her during leisure time as well as during the hours of state business. As her pregnancy progressed that winter, she was spending much more time indoors and she passed her evenings as she had always done, listening to music, chatting to her ladies, playing cards and sitting up late. The hated Riccio was now an indispensable member of these informal evening parties and the very characteristics which alienated the Scots endeared him to the Queen. He was little and amusing, droll in his ways, and he had endless tales about the personalities he had met at the continental Courts. Starved as she was of such gossip, Mary listened to him delightedly and cared little for the foolish rumours which began to circulate about their relationship. She laughed it off when she heard that people were saying Riccio was her lover.

It would have been annoying if it had not been so ridiculous. A royal Queen would never take a mere secretary into her bed and in any case the physical difference between them made the idea ludicrous. Mary was a six-foot-tall beauty and she was visibly pregnant. Riccio was tiny, misshapen, ugly and a good deal older than she. Lowminded people always gossiped in that way, she knew, and her enemies were all too ready to spread evil rumour. She and Darnley had been the subject of similar speculation in the weeks leading up to their wedding, but this time the tales were so far-fetched that she imagined no sensible person could believe them for a moment.

Unfortunately the idle gossip was to provide her enemies with the means they needed to draw Darnley into their treacherous schemes. Moray and the other Protestant Lords who had fled to England after the 'Chaseabout Raid' were anxious to return home, and in Scotland itself there were plenty of other people, eager to exploit the ill-feeling between

Darnley and Riccio for their own purposes. James, Earl of Morton, was particularly active and he was well-placed to interfere. Himself a Douglas, he made sure that Darnley's other Douglas relatives did all they could to add to the young man's jealousy. One of the King's uncles began to spend a great deal of time in his company and he lost no opportunity to fuel all Darnley's suspicions with hints that Mary was unfaithful. He sympathised with his complaints about her neglect and he urged him to seek revenge.

When they had exhausted that theme for the time being, Morton and his cronies declared indignantly that it was scandalous that the crown matrimonial was still being kept from him. More than six months had gone by since the wedding and yet, for all her former promises, Mary was still withholding it. She excluded him from the business of running the country, they said, and if anything happened to her Darnley would lose all his status. She must make arrangements right away to ensure that he would be King for as long as he lived, and that his son, by whatever wife, would one day rule Scotland.

There was little need to emphasise these points to Darnley, for he and his father were obsessed by that very subject and their dearest ambition was to found their own royal dynasty. However, no matter how her husband sulked and pleaded, no matter how often he threw tantrums and took the huff, Mary continued to ignore his demands. He was still very young, she told people, and he had yet to prove himself. Beside himself with rage, he spent more and more time with his new friends and in the early weeks of 1566 events began to move swiftly.

Parliament was due to meet in March and Moray and the rebel Lords would be charged with treason and deprived of their lands. They could not allow that to happen and so an unlikely alliance between those Lords, the Douglases and Darnley was formed. Almost everyone at Court realised that something was afoot and, by the middle of February, Sir James Melville and his friends were so concerned that they pleaded with the Queen to pardon the rebel Lords so that trouble would be averted. He had heard rumours, Sir James told her, and he was afraid of what was going to happen. Mary replied that she had heard them too, but she dismissed them as mere gossip, reminding Sir James half-humorously that although the Scots were great talkers they rarely put their bragging into effect. As for pardoning Moray and the others, she declared that she simply could not bear to have any dealings with such traitors.

In spite of her apparent unconcern, however, she must have felt uneasy for after further pleading she eventually agreed that she would at least postpone parliament. That was not all Sir James Melville's doing, of course. Messages from Queen Elizabeth on behalf of Moray had played an important part in her decision.

Had Mary kept to this plan all might have been well, but within a short space of time urgent letters from France caused her to change her mind. Her uncle the Cardinal had just returned from the Council of Trent, a gathering of leading members of the Catholic Church, and during their deliberations the Catholic Princes had decided to band themselves together with the aim of rooting out Protestantism. The Cardinal urged his

106. The Stonyhurst Reliquary, containing a holy thorn believed by Mary to be from Christ's crown of thorns and brought by her from France. The gold reliquary itself was made in the early seventeenth century. (Stonyhurst College)

niece to join them, and, apparently as a result, she decided that this would not be the moment to pardon her own Protestant rebels. Changing her mind for a second time, she announced that parliament would meet in the middle of March, as originally planned.

The Earl of Morton and his friends saw that they had no time to lose, and together with Moray and the other exiles they drew up a sinister scheme. By violent means, the Douglases would make sure that parliament would take no proceedings against the Lords. In exchange, Moray and his companions promised that they would obtain the crown matrimonial for Darnley.

It was a strange and unnatural alliance, for the very reason that Moray was in disgrace was that he had objected to Darnley marrying the Queen in the first place. All thoughts of that were now put aside, but no one trusted anyone else and the conspirators made sure that Lord Darnley signed a bond agreeing to their scheme. He was not to be allowed to declare that he had known nothing about it if anything went wrong.

The nature of the plot was well known in England before ever it was put into effect. By the middle of February Sir Thomas Randolph had been able to tell Queen Elizabeth's advisers that Darnley and his father were plotting to obtain the crown, that David Riccio would be murdered and that there was even word of a threat to Mary herself. By the end of the month he had even more details, and he reported that it was simply a matter of time

107. Gold enamelled locket with miniature portraits of Mary and her son.
(National Museums of Scotland)

108. Gold enamelled pendant set with crystal, showing Mary's royal arms: of French workmanship, about 1550–60.
(National Museums of Scotland)

before Morton and the others embarked upon their 'great attempt'.

On 7 March 1566 Mary, now in the sixth month of her pregnancy, attended the opening session of parliament. Darnley, furious at the fact that he still lacked the crown matrimonial, refused to accompany her. At that first session it was agreed that on 12 March a bill of attainder against Moray would be passed, so that he would forfeit all his possessions in Scotland. Two days after the opening meeting, the conspirators struck.

The Queen was staying at Holyrood and that Saturday evening she sat down to supper as usual in her cabinet, the little room adjoining her bedchamber. Her customary evening companions were with her: her half-sister Jean, Countess of Argyll, her half-brother Lord Robert Stewart and several members of her entourage. Robert Beaton, the Master of her

109. Holyrood Palace: general view. (Reproduced by gracious permission of Her Majesty The Queen: photograph, A. Forbes)

110. Holyrood Palace: Darnley's antechamber. (Reproduced by gracious permission of Her Majesty The Queen: photograph, A. Forbes)

111. Holyrood Palace: Darnley's bedchamber. (Reproduced by gracious permission of Her Majesty The Queen: photograph, A. Forbes)

112. Holyrood Palace: Darnley's dressingroom. (Reproduced by gracious permission of Her Majesty The Queen: photograph, A. Forbes)

Household was in attendance and so were Arthur Erskine, captain of the Guard, David Riccio himself, her French apothecary and one or two domestic servants. There was hardly space for them all in that one small chamber, but they were used to it and no doubt they enjoyed the feeling of warmth and privacy on that cold spring night.

It was Lent, but because the Queen was pregnant she had been told to eat meat and so a sustaining meal was brought in and placed on a small table with a candlestick on it. It was already dark, and the candles had been lit. The Queen took her place at the middle of the table, the Countess of Argyll seated herself at one end and David Riccio was placed at the other.

They had just started to eat when a sudden sound outside brought their happy chatter to an abrupt halt. It seemed to come from the thickness of the wall, where a narrow private stair led down from the cabinet to Darnley's apartments, which lay immediately below. The tapestry which concealed the door to the stair was lifted and there in the open doorway stood Lord Darnley himself.

Everyone stared at him in surprise. No one had been expecting him, for he and Mary avoided each other's company and he did not join her in the evenings, preferring to roam around the town with his disreputable companions. To add to the general bewilderment, he announced that he had already eaten supper, so he did not require any. However, he seemed to be in an unusually good humour for he sat down beside the Queen and put his arm playfully round her waist. They exchanged a few words, but before she could question him more closely about his reason for coming, there was another disturbance, a much louder commotion on the private stair and this time an even more startling apparition appeared in the doorway. It was Lord Ruthven, clad in full armour, his face a ghastly white.

For a moment, the people in the room imagined that they were seeing a ghost, for they all knew that for the past three months he had been ill and that very week they had been told he was lying at the point of death. According to his own account, he was so weak that he was hardly able to walk twice the length of his bedchamber unaided, but there he stood, a vengeful and alarming figure.

There was a pause while he surveyed them all in silence with his terrible gaze, then he spoke. In a voice of doom he declared,

'May it please Your Majesty to let yonder man Davie come forth of your presence, for he has been overlong here!'

Much alarmed, the Queen cried,

'What offence hath he made?'

'Great offence!' replied Lord Ruthven.

Mary now realised what was going to happen. Ruthven, her former adviser, the alleged sorcerer, had come with murderous intent. Furiously she turned to her husband, demanding what he knew about all this. Darnley replied that he did not know anything at all, and so she turned back to the intruder and ordered him to leave at once or be condemned as a traitor. If Riccio had been guilty of any offence, she said, she would punish him, but it would be done legally.

Lord Ruthven ignored her. Looking at Darnley, he said warningly,

113. Holyrood Palace: the door to the private stair between Darnley's apartments and Mary's. (Reproduced by gracious permission of Her Majesty The Queen: photograph, A. Forbes)

'Sir, take the Queen's Majesty your sovereign and wife to you.'

Mary rose to her feet in dismay, Darnley seized her in his arms and Riccio darted swiftly behind her to cower in terror in a window embrasure at her back, clinging to the pleats of her gown. At the same moment, her attendants leaped into action. Lord Robert, Arthur Erskine, Robert Beaton, the French apothecary and one of the grooms all sprang forward as if to take Lord Ruthven but he pulled out his pistol and waved them back.

'Lay not hands on me,' he cried, 'for I will not be handled!'

As he spoke, the door from the main staircase burst open and the Earl of Morton's men rushed into the little room. In the confusion which followed the table was overturned, toppling towards the wall, plates and cups

114. Holyrood Palace: Mary's audience chamber. (Reproduced by gracious permission of Her Majesty The Queen: photograph, A. Forbes)

115. Holyrood Palace: Mary's bedchamber. (Reproduced by gracious permission of Her Majesty The Queen: photograph, A. Forbes)

crashing to the floor. The Countess of Argyll snatched up the candlestick before it too could fall and plunge the chamber into darkness.

Lord Ruthven now seized hold of Riccio, and George Douglas, Darnley's uncle, snatched Darnley's dagger from his belt and stabbed the little Italian. According to the Queen's description of that night's events, this first blow was struck over her own shoulder, while a pistol was pressed to her stomach, then they dragged Riccio away.

'Justice! Justice!' he screamed, 'Save my life, Madame, save me!'

It was too late. In Mary's words, they 'dragged David with great cruelty forth from our cabinet and at the entrance of our chamber dealt him 56 dagger wounds'. At Darnley's command, the body was then hurled down the staircase, dragged into the porter's lodge and thrown across a coffer. As the porter's servant stripped Riccio of his fine clothing he commented,

'This hath been his destiny, for upon this chest was his first bed when he entered into this place and now here he lieth again, a very ingrate [ungrateful] and misknowing knave.'

When Darnley went back into the supper room, Mary exclaimed,

'My Lord! Why have you caused to do this wicked deed to me, considering I took you from a base estate and made you my husband? What offence have I made you, that ye should have done me such shame?'

'Since yon fellow Davie fell in credit and familiarity with Your Majesty,' he retorted, 'Ye regarded me not, neither treated me nor entertained me after your wonted fashion, for every day before dinner and after dinner ye would come to my chamber and pass time with me and this long time ye have not done so, and when I come to Your Majesty's chamber ye bear me little company except Davie had been the third marrow [companion] and after supper Your Majesty hath a use to sit at the cards with the said Davie till one or two of the clock after midnight, and this is the entertainment that I have had of you this long time!'

Furiously, Mary replied that if he did not like the way she treated him it was all his own doing, and, she declared,

'I shall never be your wife nor lie with you nor shall never like well till I cause you have as sore a heart as I have presently!'

At that point a loud groan from Lord Ruthven interrupted their argument and they turned to see him sink down on a nearby chest and call for wine. Now that the action was over, he was on the verge of collapse. A frightened servant ran away for a cup and as he drank the Queen stood over him, asking him sarcastically,

'Is *this* your sickness, Lord Ruthven?' then she told him that if either she or the child she was carrying were harmed as a result of that night's work, she had many powerful friends who would avenge her.

A sudden commotion outside attracted their attention, for the Provost of Edinburgh had got word that there was something amiss and he had arrived in the courtyard with a crowd of townspeople. Mary tried to go to the window, but Darnley prevented her. Instead, he leaned out and told them all to go home. Desperately, the Queen began to scream for help, but Lord Lindsay stopped her, snarling that he would 'cut her in collops' if she dared to make a move.

Half-hysterical now, she asked over and over what had become of Riccio.

'It shall be dear blood to some of you if his be spilt,' she cried, but it was not until much later that one of her own ladies brought her the news that her secretary was dead.

'How do you know?' the Queen asked, weeping.

'I have seen his body,' was the reply.

At that, Mary dried her eyes.

'No more tears now,' she said. 'I will think upon revenge.'

6
PRINCE JAMES

THE QUEEN spent that night alone, except for the Dowager Countess of Huntly. Lord Ruthven had departed downstairs at last, taking Darnley with him. The Douglases held the Palace and none of the Queen's attendants was allowed to go to her. Lord Semple's son stood guard over Riccio's chamber, keeping out anyone who fancied searching for the gold and silver which were believed to be hidden within. Elsewhere in the building, Mary's friends protected themselves as best they could. The Earl of Huntly and the Earl of Bothwell, fearing for their lives, escaped through back windows. If she were to survive, the Queen would have to save herself.

Next morning, Lord Darnley awoke in a very different frame of mind from his bravado of recent weeks. It had been all very well to urge the murder of Riccio, but the actual violence of the night before had terrified him. Ruthven and Lindsay were desperate men who might do away with him next. Frantic with fear for his own safety, he could only think of turning to the person who had given him support and encouragement in the past: the Queen herself.

He appeared in her doorway at eight o'clock that Sunday morning and at once flung himself on his knees, weeping loudly and saying through his tears, 'Ah, my Mary,' which had been his way of addressing her in happier days.

'I am bound to confess at this time,' he sobbed, 'though now it is too late, that I have failed in my duty towards you. . . .'

Miserably, he said that he was young, and he had been tricked by wicked traitors.

'I ask you, my Mary, to have pity on me, have pity on our child, have pity on yourself', he went on. 'Unless you take some means to prevent it we are all ruined, and that speedily', and he produced the bond he had signed with the conspirators and handed it to her.

'Sire,' she replied, 'Within the last twenty four hours you have done me such a wrong that neither the recollection of our early friendship nor all the hope you can give me of the future can ever make me forget it'. In the past, she said, she had always cared more for his welfare than he had done himself.

'You say you are sorry for what you have done,' she added, 'and this gives me some comfort. Yet I cannot but think that you are driven to it rather by necessity than led by any sentiment of true and sincere affection. Had I offended you as deeply as can be imagined you could not have discovered how to avenge yourself upon me with greater disgrace or cruelty.'

In reply to her reproaches, he poured out a torrent of remorse and pleaded for her sympathy.

'Since you have placed us both on the brink of the precipice, you must now deliberate how we shall escape the peril,' she told him, but she knew that she would have to devise the plan for their escape. He was incapable of helping.

By questioning him, she discovered that the conspirators meant to take her to Stirling Castle and keep her prisoner there until her child was born. After that, the Lords would rule on behalf of the infant and she would remain a captive until she died. She realised that at all costs she must avoid being taken from Holyrood, but at over six months pregnant she could not hope to make a daring escape. Instead, she would take advantage of her condition and pretend that her labour was starting. They would never dare to move her if they believed that the child was about to arrive.

That afternoon, therefore, she pretended to be in great pain and so convincing was she that Lord Ruthven and the others were forced to summon a midwife for her. Desperately playing for time, she managed to deceive the woman who came to attend her, and she succeeded in communicating with Bothwell and Huntly. They had concocted a plan whereby she would climb down a rope ladder, but she sent them word that it would never work: even if she did manage to get out of her window she would be seen, for there were guards in the room above. Instead, Huntly and the others should wait for her at Seton. She would find another means of escape.

As she waited, feigning illness, the Earl of Moray and the rebel Lords arrived back in Edinburgh. That same morning, a proclamation cancelling the forthcoming parliament had been issued in Darnley's name and they were safe from prosecution. Darnley himself greeted them, and then they went to Morton's house to have supper and hear at first hand all that had been happening. No sooner had they sat down to their meal than one of the Queen's ushers arrived, summoning Moray to her presence.

When he arrived at Holyrood, she welcomed him more gladly than either of them would have believed possible a few months before. She did not know that he was deeply involved with Morton and the rest and she had deliberately decided to greet him cordially for she wanted to detach him from the other conspirators. Apart from that, though, as soon as she saw his familiar figure, the remembrance of their past affection drove all her former resentment from her mind. She went across to him, embraced him and kissed him warmly. If only he had been at home, she told him tearfully, he would never have 'suffered her to be so uncourteously handled'. For his part, he was equally affected, his anger temporarily replaced by pity and concern when he saw her distress, and at her words he was 'so moved that the tears fell from his eyes'.

The following afternoon he came to see her again, but this time it was a formal visit, in company with Morton and the others. They wished to obtain her pardon for their part in Riccio's murder. This had already been a source of new argument between the Queen and Darnley. He was all for pardoning the conspirators right away, for he naively believed that this was the only way out of their dangerous situation. Mary was too much of a realist to trust in such a simple solution, and in any event she could not bring herself to forgive the men who had murdered her secretary within days of the dreadful crime.

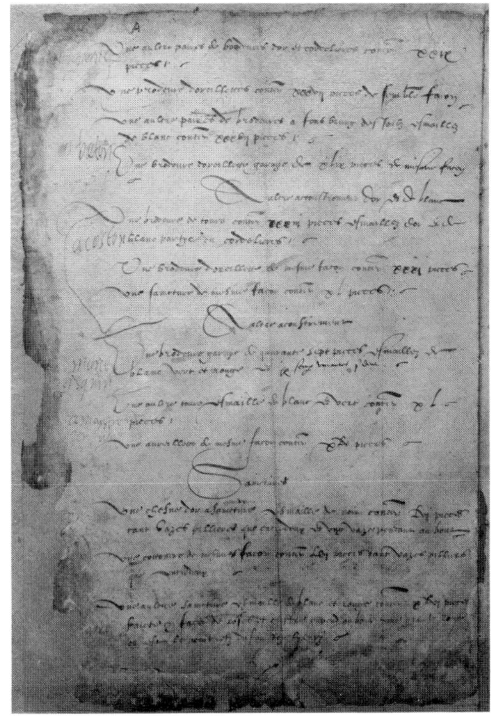

116. List of bequests made by Mary before the birth of Prince James: her handwriting can be seen in the margin on the left, with the names of the recipients—'Beton' and others.
(Scottish Record Office)

'My conscience will never allow me to promise what I do not mean to perform,' she told him, 'nor can I bring myself to tell a falsehood even to those men who have betrayed me so villainously.'

Even so, she recognised that she could not refuse to pardon them, for that would have invited disaster. She had therefore told her husband that, since he was so far committed to them, he could tell them what he liked, but she would not be held responsible for any guarantees he gave. As she had expected, he had gone at once to Moray and arranged this meeting.

The Lords filed into her antechamber and knelt down before her, Morton, she observed, on the very spot where Riccio had been stabbed. He was a tough, truculent man with a bushy red beard and she had always particularly disliked his coarse and brutal manner. Now he was acting as the Lords' spokesman, while Moray, who had risen to his feet again very quickly, stood listening in silence.

When Morton had finished asking her to pardon them, the Queen spoke. She could not do so at once, she said, but if, by their future behaviour, they tried to blot out the past, then 'I give you my word,' she said, 'that on my part I will endeavour to forget what you have done.' With that they would have to be content.

It was not enough for them, of course, and Moray launched into a long harangue. She must learn to forgive, he told her, and he spoke at great length about the virtues of clemency. The Queen retorted tartly that ever since her earliest youth her subjects had given her ample opportunity for practising that particular virtue. Feeling her anger mounting, she knew that she must end the audience before she said something she would regret, and so she pretended to be seized by a violent pain. Calling for her midwife, she allowed the woman to assist her to her bedchamber.

Her husband was left behind to try to allay the suspicions of the conspirators. Not surprisingly, this was difficult and they demanded proof that Mary really would pardon them. Darnley assured them fervently that she would keep her word, but in the end he only managed to get rid of them by telling them that they could draw up a document which she would sign.

Still grumbling resentfully, the Lords withdrew and composed a set of articles. They gave the paper to Darnley, who promised that he would take it to her. He disappeared upstairs but when he came back it was to tell them that the Queen was far too ill to read anything. However, she would be sure to study it and put her name to it in the morning. There was nothing more they could do. Still extremely suspicious, they marched back to Morton's house, had supper and eventually retired to bed.

Down at the Palace, Mary and Darnley were waiting anxiously until the whole house fell silent. Even at the last moment they had a fierce argument when Darnley announced that they must take his father with them when they escaped, for Lennox was terrified of being left in the hands of the murderers. The Queen refused point blank. She had always treated the Earl of Lennox with the utmost respect, she said, and in fact she had often rebuked her husband for his own attitude to his father, but this was different. Lennox had so far forgotten himself as to join the traitors, and he deserved anything that happened to him. Darnley lapsed into a sullen silence.

At last, when one o'clock came, Mary judged that the time was right. Silently she led her husband down the little staircase to his quarters, along past chambers occupied by her own faithful French servants, through store rooms and wine cellars and finally out at the back of the Palace and across the cemetery to the gate where Arthur Erskine and a small group of friends were waiting with horses. Erskine took the Queen up behind him, her husband mounted his own horse and cautiously they set off.

Darnley was terrified that they would be followed, and when they approached Seton Palace he mistook their waiting supporters for the enemy.

'Come on! Come on!' he screamed hysterically at Mary. 'By God's blood, they will murder both you and me if they can catch us', and he lashed at his own horse and hers until she had to plead with him to remember her condition. He replied crudely that if she lost this child they could get others. Worn out, Mary told him to ride on and save himself. This he did, without more ado.

Five hours after leaving Holyrood, the Queen arrived at Dunbar Castle, exhausted and dishevelled but unharmed. There, weary though she was, and plagued by bouts of sickness, she dictated long letters to her friends abroad and to Queen Elizabeth describing Riccio's murder and asking for help. Back in Edinburgh, the conspirators were aghast when they discovered that she had escaped, and Lord Lennox was furious at having been left behind. Mary's own supporters at once began rallying to her side and when the rebel Lords realised that Darnley had deserted them and

117. *Mary, Queen of Scots, and Lord Darnley* by an unknown artist. (The National Trust, at Hardwick Hall, Derbyshire: photograpn, National Trust)

was reconciled with his wife, they knew that they were defeated. Morton, Lindsay and Ruthven rode for England, where Ruthven died soon afterwards. Maitland, who had also been involved, departed for the safety of the Highlands and John Knox, who had certainly supported the murder, made a hasty retreat to the west of Scotland.

Seeing that her enemies were in disarray, the Queen knew that she could return to Edinburgh and she set off for the capital on 18 March. She shuddered away from the notion of staying at Holyrood, where she had been all too vulnerable to attack, and instead she lodged with Lord Herries in the High Street. There, in the centre of town, surrounded by the ordinary people, she felt safe.

The day after her return, she sent a message to Moray indicating that she was willing to come to terms with those who had been involved in the 'Chaseabout Raid'. For the murderers of Riccio, however, there would be no forgiveness and that same day she summoned Morton, Ruthven and almost seventy others to appear before herself, Darnley and the Privy Council. She would continue her successful policy of dividing the Lords.

As for Darnley, his one thought was to save himself. He was terrified that his former friends would take revenge on him for deserting them, and he was still going about claiming that he had been entirely ignorant of their intentions. He admitted only that he had encouraged Moray to come back without the Queen's permission. This served to infuriate the conspirators still further, and they lost no time in sending the Queen a copy of the bond he had signed and the detailed articles of agreement they had drawn up together.

If Morton and his friends hoped that the Queen would express horror and punish her husband for his part in Riccio's murder, they were doomed to disappointment. She already knew the extent of his involvement, for he was never able to keep a secret, and although she had been shocked and deeply disgusted by his behaviour, he was her husband, the father of her coming child, and, as she had told him before they escaped from the Palace, that meant that she could never abandon him, whatever the circumstances. She understood him and she saw only too well what had happened. His weakness and his pride had been his downfall. Stronger, desperate men had played upon his vanity and dragged him into their schemes. He, like a foolish, spoiled child, had been in many ways their victim and even in her anger at his treachery she was able to feel some pity for him. She had raised him up to the foremost position in the land but he was too shallow and too immature to sustain such a place in her kingdom. Now he and she would have to live with the consequences of his folly, and they would have to make the best of it.

At the forefront of her mind was her coming child, and she devoted herself that spring to trying to restore peace and stability to the country. The principal murderers had fled, but four lesser men were condemned to death, although two of them were pardoned on the scaffold by the Queen's own command. In early April she gave orders for Riccio's body to be exhumed from the common grave in Holyrood cemetery where he had hastily been buried, and he was given a solemn funeral service in the Chapel Royal. Less than a fortnight later, his eighteen-year-old brother Joseph arrived in Scotland with the French ambassador and was appointed secretary in David's place.

For greater safety, Mary now moved into Edinburgh Castle. She was afraid that the Lords still planned to seize her child as soon as the infant was born and, because she feared that she might die in childbirth, she was anxious to unite her own supporters so that they would safeguard the baby's future. She summoned Moray to Court and forgave him for his part in the 'Chaseabout Raid'. By the end of the month, she had succeeded in reconciling Moray, Bothwell and Huntly to each other. The only person who would not join in the general pacification was her own husband, and, as Sir James Melville observed, he 'past up and down on his own and few durst bear him company'.

Now that the immediate danger to his life was over, he had reverted to his old ways and Moray spoke of him angrily as 'a young fool and proud tyrant'. The Queen tried to put on a show of normality when strangers were present, but there were rumours that she would seek a divorce, and early in May one English visitor declared that Mary hated her husband so much that people thought he could not safely remain in Scotland.

The date of the Queen's confinement was fast approaching, and on 3 June she took to her chamber to await the birth. Margaret Asteane, her midwife, was in attendance and Mary took the precaution of sending over to Dunfermline for relics of St Margaret, which she hoped would see her safely through the ordeal ahead. While she waited, she drew up her will. If

118. Edinburgh Castle, from the South. (Historic Buildings and Monuments, SDD)

119. Edinburgh Castle: the room where James VI was born.
(Historic Buildings and Monuments, SDD)

she died but her child survived, everything was to go to the child. If the baby died too her valuables were to be divided up. Her most splendid jewels would go to the Scottish crown, to be the property of future Kings and Queens, in memory of herself and, she said, of the alliance between Scotland and the house of Lorraine.

Apart from that major gift, there were dozens of lesser bequests to her French and Scottish relatives. The Cardinal of Lorraine was to be sent a fine emerald ring, her aunts, cousins and godchildren in France would receive various pearls, rubies and diamonds, the Earl and Countess of Moray and the Countess of Argyll would fall heir to other jewels. Nor was Lord Darnley forgotten. No fewer than twenty-five items were left to him, including a diamond ring enamelled in red. 'It was with this that I was

120. The date of Prince James's birth, painted on the wall of the room where he was born, in Edinburgh Castle.
(Historic Buildings and Monuments, SDD)

married,' the Queen wrote. 'I leave it to the King, who gave it to me.' In like manner, a jewel containing ten rubies and a pearl which David Riccio had once presented to her would be handed over to his brother Joseph. Her ladies, equerries, Arthur Erskine and the other members of her inner household were remembered too.

On 18 June the Queen went into labour in the small room which can still be seen in Edinburgh Castle to this day. As her contractions increased she called out that she wished she had never married. St Margaret's relics seemed to be doing no good and she prayed aloud to God to save her child rather than herself. Moray and Argyll, who had been allowed to lodge in the Castle, waited anxiously nearby and the Countess of Atholl obligingly tried to help by using sorcery to transfer Mary's pains to Lady Reres instead. This ingenious attempt met with no success either, but at last, between ten and eleven the next morning, the baby was born: a fine, healthy son.

Tired and weak though she was, the Queen made a point of summoning her husband to her chamber. There, in front of her assembled household, she showed him the baby.

'My Lord,' she said, 'God has given you and me a son, begotten by none but you.'

Drawing back the covers from the child's face, she continued solemnly,

'Here I protest to God, as I shall answer to him at the great day of Judgment, that this is your son and no other man's son. I am desirous that all here, with ladies and others, bear witness.' Then, in a bitter aside, she added,

'For he is so much your own son that I fear it will be the worse for him hereafter.'

Darnley's sullen response was only what people had learned to expect from him, but outside there was great rejoicing: for the first time in almost thirty years, Scotland had a male heir to the throne. The Castle guns were fired in salute, more than five hundred bonfires were lit in Edinburgh alone and a special service of thanksgiving was held in the Church of St Giles.

As soon as the good news was announced, Sir James Melville was sent to London to tell Queen Elizabeth. He arrived four days later, on Sunday, to find the English Queen dancing after supper. Sir William Cecil went

121. *John, Earl of Mar,* hereditary guardian of Prince James, by an unknown artist from an earlier painting. (Scottish National Portrait Gallery)

over and whispered to her that a Prince had been born, and at once the atmosphere in the room changed. Elizabeth sat down pensively with her cheek on her hand and said nothing at all until she suddenly burst out 'that the Queen of Scotland was lighter of a fair son, and that she was but a barren stock.' The feeling of personal rivalry with Mary was never far from her mind, nor could she forget that this baby had Tudor blood in his veins.

Ironically, Mary's own position was weakened by the birth of her son. There was nothing the Scottish nobility liked better than a royal minority, when they could vie with each other for possession of an infant King and when the person who won control of the baby could govern the country himself in all but regal state. The Queen was therefore nervous about her own safety and even more worried about her child, whom she named James, after her father. Breaking with tradition, she arranged for his cradle to be placed in her own bedchamber, and she often watched over him herself.

Darnley was certainly no help, and indeed his rash behaviour added to the danger. He roved around the town with his unsuitable companions, and he had a foolish habit of bathing in the sea in secluded coves. Knowing

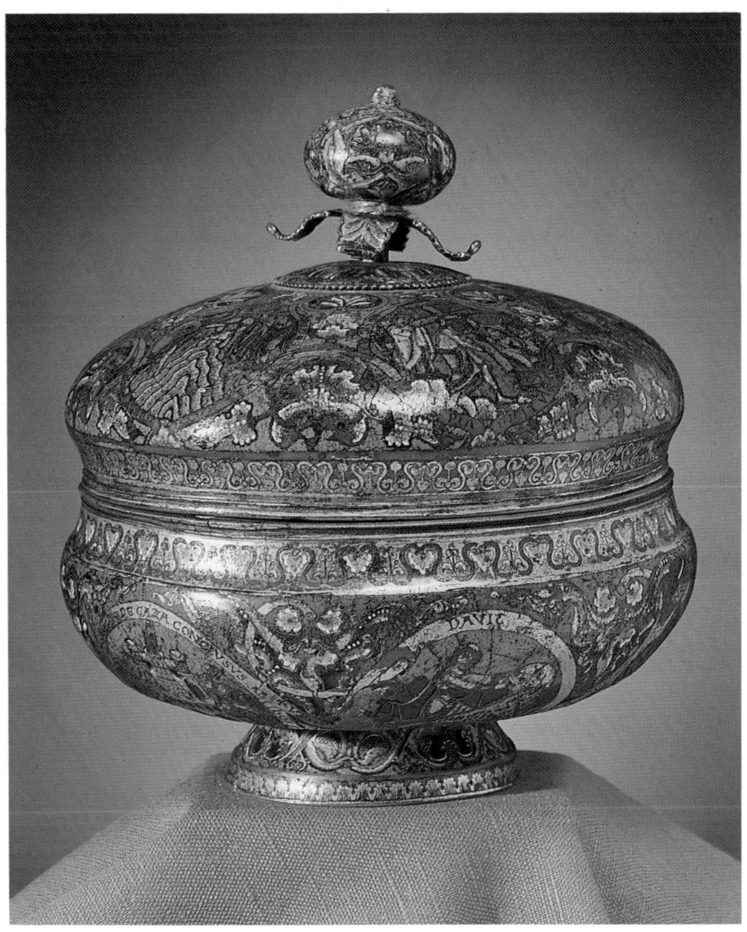

122. The Balfour ciborium, a twelfth-century enamelled ecclesiastical cup, probably the one which belonged to Mary and is listed in her inventories.
(By courtesy of the Board of Trustees of the Victoria and Albert Museum)

how her Lords hated him, the Queen was afraid he would be attacked, but he had no care for either his own safety or hers. He would return to the Castle at all hours of the night, which meant that the gates had to be opened up for him, and Mary lived in fear of her enemies taking advantage of his irregular comings and goings to force their way in.

By her own account, she tried to be with him as much as she could, to prevent him from making mischief and she gave in to his demands that she should sleep with him again. After all, he was her husband and she could not refuse him. However, the strain of keeping watch on him, wondering what trouble he would make next, was taking its toll and she was quick-tempered and on edge, ready to rebuke anyone who as much as spoke pleasantly to Darnley.

At the end of July, Lord Mar persuaded her to go for a short rest to his house at Alloa, but Darnley took exception to that and they quarrelled again during a stag hunt at Traquair. That August, she decided to move her son to the greater safety of Stirling Castle, where he would live under the protection of Lord Mar, with his own household. She escorted the Prince there personally, and while she was in Stirling she received

123. Doune Castle, at that time a royal castle. (Historic Buildings and Monuments, SDD)

Maitland of Lethington back into favour. With his return, her campaign to restore peace and order was almost complete.

Unfortunately, Darnley now let it be known that he was thinking of leaving the country. Because his wife did not treat him properly, he would go and live in France on her revenues there. This announcement brought Mary and her courtiers to a new pitch of exasperation with him. Although they would have been only too glad to be quit of him, the Lords could not allow him to carry out a plan which would have been such a public affront to the Queen. The Privy Council went so far as to remind him in public that he ought to thank God for giving him such a wise and virtuous wife, and Mary took him by the hand in front of them all and begged him to say if she had given him any cause to leave the country. He could give no sensible reply, and she despaired of his unreasonable behaviour.

In October, she planned to travel through Teviotdale, dispensing justice. Darnley was expected to accompany her, but he refused to go. He was still boasting that he would leave the country, and he spent a lot of time composing lengthy letters to France, Spain, the Pope and anyone else who occurred to him, complaining that Mary was not a good Roman

124. Mary, Queen of Scots House, Jedburgh, probably a slightly later building on the site of the house where she stayed during her serious illness. (Photograph, Michael Brooks)

Catholic. This, coming from a self-confessed Protestant, was strange stuff. Mary's journey to Teviotdale had to go ahead with or without him and the journey began badly. The Queen was feeling ill, troubled with a pain in her side, then before they had gone far, word came that the Earl of Bothwell had been seriously hurt in a skirmish and was lying at death's door in Hermitage Castle.

The Queen was distressed, for he was one of her most loyal supporters and she asked to be kept informed of his progress. Five days later, when she heard that he was recovering, she decided to go from Jedburgh to the Hermitage to see him. Accompanied by the Earl of Moray and a large group of courtiers, she rode twenty-five miles across country to his stark, awe-inspiring fortress. There, she and the Lords spoke to him for an hour or two. They could not spend the night at the castle, for it was not equipped for guests, so they had to ride back to Jedburgh that same evening and the double journey proved too much for Mary. Her health had been poor since the birth of Prince James, and now she suffered an alarming illness. She began to have convulsions and, fearing that she was about to die, she sent for her Lords to tell them her last wishes. Darnley

125. Hermitage Castle, Bothwell's Border stronghold, visited by Mary during his recovery from his injuries. (Historic Buildings and Monuments, SDD)

was not to be allowed to seize the crown. Her son was to be the next King and he was to be brought up carefully and kept away from evil company. Reminding Moray that she had never persecuted the Protestants, she asked him to show similar tolerance to the Catholics when she had gone.

She really seemed to be on the point of death, for on 25 October she lay on her bed unconscious, her limbs stiff and cold. Only the presence of mind of her French physician saved her. Hastily wrapping bandages tightly round her legs, he forced open her mouth and poured a little wine

126. Craigmillar Castle, where Mary and her Lords discussed the problem of Darnley.
(Historic Buildings and Monuments, SDD)

between her lips. When she seemed to revive slightly, he managed to make her swallow a medicinal draught, and after vomiting she began slowly to recover. As soon as he was well enough, Bothwell came to see her but Darnley did not appear until a week after that.

Mary herself blamed stress for her mysterious illness, and she said as much at the time, telling the Lords that the trouble her husband caused her was the cause of her sickness. Similarly, Maitland told the Scottish ambassador in France that Darnley 'has recompensed her with such ingratitude, and misuses himself so far towards her, that it is a heartbreak to her to think that he should be her husband, and how to be free of him she sees no way out'. She remained unwell for several weeks and it was only after she had vomited blood that she really began to feel better. Even so, she remained deeply depressed. After receiving one of Darnley's complaining letters, she exclaimed to Moray and Maitland that 'unless she was free of him in some way she had no pleasure to live, and if she could find no other remedy, she would slay herself'. This mood persisted throughout November, and she was often heard to remark,

'I would wish to be dead!'

She and the Lords were staying at Craigmillar Castle, on the outskirts of Edinburgh, and there they had long discussions about the problem of her husband. Usually, the easiest way of ending a marriage was to have it annulled by claiming that the husband and wife were too closely related

127. Sixteenth-century silver rosary crucifix found at Craigmillar Castle. The ebony backing is nineteenth-century. (National Museums of Scotland)

and had married without knowing that they were within the forbidden degrees. In this instance, the Queen had actually obtained a papal dispensation allowing her to wed her cousin and she had an even more important reason for not seeking an annulment. If she did so, her son would be declared illegitimate. She could never agree to that, for he would then lose his position as heir to the throne.

Another possibility was a Catholic divorce. The only ground for that was adultery, and Darnley had been openly unfaithful, having a series of casual affairs with Edinburgh prostitutes. It would be easy enough to concoct some evidence of a longstanding relationship outside marriage, but even divorce had its drawbacks. It did not end a marriage completely. The husband and wife did not live together any more, but they were not allowed to remarry, for in the eyes of God they remained partners.

The Lords, of course, had a different solution in view. No one actually put into words the thought that Darnley could be removed as David Riccio had been, but that was the notion in most of their minds, and Maitland apparently told the Queen that, if he and his friends could arrive at some method of eliminating her husband without any disadvantage to the Prince, the Earl of Moray would be willing to 'look through his fingers' at whatever was arranged.

When this was suggested, the Queen was appalled. She told them at once that they must do nothing whereby any spot would be laid upon her honour or her conscience. She could not possibly countenance a violent solution to her difficulties. No matter how troublesome Darnley was personally, she could never condone a threat to the safety of the man who was not only her lawful husband but the monarch of a kingdom.

They argued for several days, and in the end the Queen and her Lords seem to have arrived at differing conclusions. Without her knowledge and

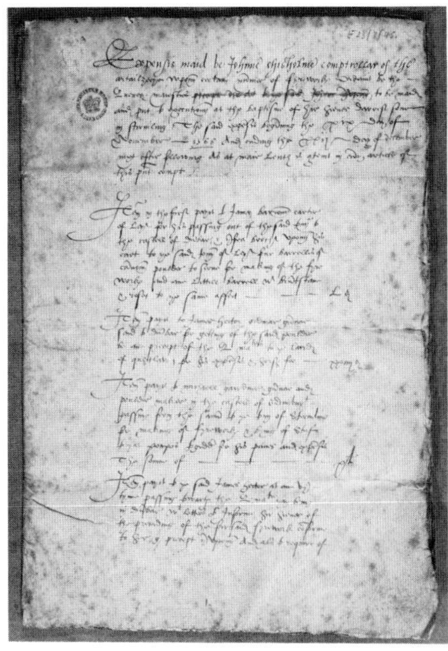

128. Account for the fireworks at Prince James's baptism. (Scottish Record Office)

in complete disregard of her instructions, the courtiers had decided to go ahead with a scheme to kill Darnley, believing that she would be so relieved once he was gone that she would do nothing to punish them. Mary, for her part, now had to decide either to divorce her husband for adultery or seek a reconciliation. At that point, she probably inclined towards the former, but whatever her decision she left Craigmillar with a sense of relief at having aired her feelings. Unsatisfactory though the situation might be, at least her Lords showed no signs of banding together with Darnley against her.

She travelled through to Stirling, where Prince James was about to be baptised. She had planned every detail of the ceremony with loving care, and she had selected suitably important godparents for this infant who would one day be King of Scots. There were to be three: the King of France, the Duke of Savoy and Queen Elizabeth of England. Her invitation to Elizabeth had brought a pleasing response. She would not come north in person, but she sent a gift of unusual magnificence. It was a huge gold font, enamelled and set with precious stones. It was so large that the baby could be totally immersed in it and it weighed three hundred and thirty three ounces. Everyone who saw it was impressed: for once, Queen Elizabeth's notorious meanness had been set aside.

The only sour note was struck by Darnley himself. When he heard that his wife had chosen Queen Elizabeth as a godparent he was furious. Elizabeth never had given her consent or approval to his marriage and he regarded her as his mortal enemy. He took Mary's selection of her as a personal insult, there was another violent quarrel between them, and he marched off to his own apartments and refused to join in any of the celebrations.

The christening went ahead without him, of course. The service was a

Catholic one, conducted by Archbishop Hamilton, with three Scottish bishops in attendance. The Comte de Brienne, as proxy for the King of France, carried the baby in procession from Mary's apartments to the Chapel Royal, followed by members of the Scottish Catholic nobility. Queen Elizabeth's representative, the Earl of Bedford, should have held the Prince up for baptism but he was a staunch Protestant so he refused even to enter the Chapel. Instead, the baby's aunt, the Countess of Argyll, took him from the Comte, thereby earning herself a handsome gift from Elizabeth and a stern censure from the Protestant ministers. Although Bedford did not take part in the ceremony he waited at the chapel door in company with three distinguished friends, each of whom was wearing a special suit purchased for the occasion at the Queen's expense. The Earl of Moray was in green, the Earl of Argyll wore red and the Earl of Bothwell favoured blue.

At about five o'clock in the afternoon the service ended and the congregation adjourned to the Great Hall for a lavish supper, followed by the usual dancing and masques. The rejoicing went on beyond that, for two days later an elaborate banquet preceded an exciting fireworks display which had taken forty days to prepare and cost almost two hundred pounds.

While all this was going on, Darnley skulked in his apartments, trying in vain to make contact with the French and Spanish ambassadors to whom he hoped to complain. The one refused to see him, the other was told by Mary that her husband had no wish to speak with him. Unable to pour out his grievances, he was more isolated that ever and on Christmas Eve he left Stirling and retreated to Glasgow, his own part of the country, while the Queen rode off to visit Lord Drummond at his castle near Crieff. Among her companions was the Earl of Bothwell.

129. *Prince James* (James VI) as a child, by Arnold Bronckorst. (Scottish National Portrait Gallery)

INRI

7
KIRK O'FIELD

IN THE Earl of Bothwell, Mary felt she had found that rare phenomenon in Scottish politics, someone who was completely loyal to the crown and would remain so. He had been of service to her mother and since her own return to Scotland he had given ample evidence of his fidelity. She admired bravery always and in her mind at least his courage was without question. She may not have admitted it to herself, but she probably felt sexually drawn to him as well. He was about seven years older than she and several inches shorter, but he was tough, muscular and handsome in a swarthy way. Moreover, he knew how to charm women. He had a string of discarded mistresses and no desire to marry until the previous winter when grave financial difficulties had forced him to wed Lady Jean Gordon, the Earl of Huntly's wealthy sister. He was sophisticated enough to be a pleasant companion, and he spoke French, for he had spent a considerable time in France. Apart from that, the reckless rashness which so annoyed his contemporaries appealed to Mary, who had too long endured the feckless foibles of Lord Darnley. She took Bothwell's downright manner and his lack of artifice to be signs of his honesty and she much preferred his brusqueness to the obsequious double dealing of some of her other Lords.

Unfortunately, they did not see him that way. They complained that he was over-ambitious, vainglorious and hot-headed. They were intensely jealous, of course, and as soon as they realised that Mary relied upon him, they began to spread unpleasant rumours to the effect that the Queen and Bothwell enjoyed a relationship far more intimate than that of monarch and subject.

In fact, no one has found any evidence that Mary was ever unfaithful to Darnley, and if she was thinking now of ending her marriage, she was inspired not by lust for another man, but by sheer weariness of spirit at her husband's behaviour. Three days after her son's baptism, she made a lavish grant of funds to the Protestant Church. It seemed as if she was seeking their support. Three days after that, she gave back to Archbishop Hamilton the powers he would need to grant her a divorce. As the traditional enemy of the Lennoxes, a Hamilton would be eager to oblige, whereas it would have been much more difficult to persuade the Pope to do as she wished.

The very next day, she gave in to the Earl of Moray's long expressed desire that she should pardon the murderers of Riccio. To do so was to go against her own natural feelings, but it would win her Moray's loyalty in the coming crisis and it would bring Morton and the others back to Scotland where she could keep an eye on them. If they were allowed to lurk in England, it was all too likely that Darnley and Lennox would seek their help.

In spite of her precautions, there was an immediate outcry, not because

130. Gold crucifix reputed to have belonged to Mary. (Reproduced by permission of His Grace the Duke of Norfolk and the Baroness Herries)

people loved her husband and could not bear to see him dishonoured, but because she had restored Archbishop Hamilton. The Protestants took this as a dangerous threat to their own religion and Moray warned her that if she was to avoid serious trouble she must revoke her commission to the Archbishop. At the same time, her continental friends were sending urgent messages telling her that she must not go ahead with the divorce. If she did, she would alienate the English Catholics and Darnley would become the focus of every plot against her.

Bitterly, the Queen came to the conclusion that although divorce might ease her personal unhappiness, it would be far too damaging politically. During the first week of January she removed the Archbishop's powers again. She would not, after all, divorce Darnley. Instead, the only way left to her was to attempt a reconciliation, reassert her influence over him and make absolutely sure this time that he was never again used against her by her enemies.

Even as she wrestled with the problem of what to do next, Darnley himself had become the centre of a personal drama. On the very day he left

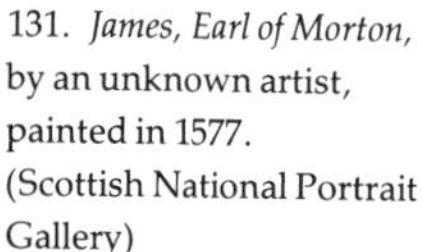

131. *James, Earl of Morton,* by an unknown artist, painted in 1577. (Scottish National Portrait Gallery)

Stirling for Glasgow, he was taken violently ill and his doctors diagnosed smallpox, which was raging in the west at the time. It has since been suggested that he was really suffering from syphilis, but while this may have been perfectly true, neither the Queen nor any of his friends at the time thought that venereal disease was the trouble. At first, indeed, Mary did not seem to take the news too seriously. Perhaps she believed that it was just another of his ploys to gain her attention. However, within a few days it became evident that he really was dangerously ill, and so she sent her own doctor to him.

She did not go to visit him in person until the second half of January. She later made the excuse that she had injured herself in a fall from her horse, but it is more likely that she did not want to see him until she had made up her mind about their future relationship. While she hesitated, further evidence of the need for a reconciliation appeared in the form of alarming rumours from London. Darnley was plotting against her, she was told by reliable sources, and it seemed clearer than ever that the only way to end his involvement in such dangerous schemes was to attach him to herself once more. On 20 January therefore she travelled through to Glasgow.

Her husband presented a pitiable sight, lying in bed, weak and emaciated, his face concealed by a taffeta mask so that visitors should not see how the disease had ravaged his pretty features. Mary had always felt a strong, protective instinct towards him and that may have made the prospect of a reconciliation more possible. At any rate, she spoke kindly to

132. Aberdour Castle, home of the Earl of Morton. (Historic Buildings and Monuments, SDD)

133. Tantallon Castle, held by the Earl of Morton on behalf of his nephew. (Historic Buildings and Monuments, SDD)

him and told him that she was willing to take him back to Edinburgh with her and there resume their married life once he was recovered.

He was huffy, of course, and nervous about leaving his father's care for he was terrified of Moray and the other Lords, fearing that they would revenge themselves on him for his desertion of their cause. However, the Queen convinced him that she would protect him in the future as she had done in the past and she promised that he would have no more cause to claim that she neglected him. He was reassured, and he was soon pouring out all the rumours he had heard about plots to kill her.

By the end of January he was fit to travel. He was placed carefully on a horse litter and together they began the journey eastwards. Mary had given orders that Craigmillar Castle should be prepared to receive them. She could not possibly have him stay at Holyrood, for she had just installed her son there and she could not risk exposing the baby to the infection. Craigmillar was only a short distance from the capital and it was

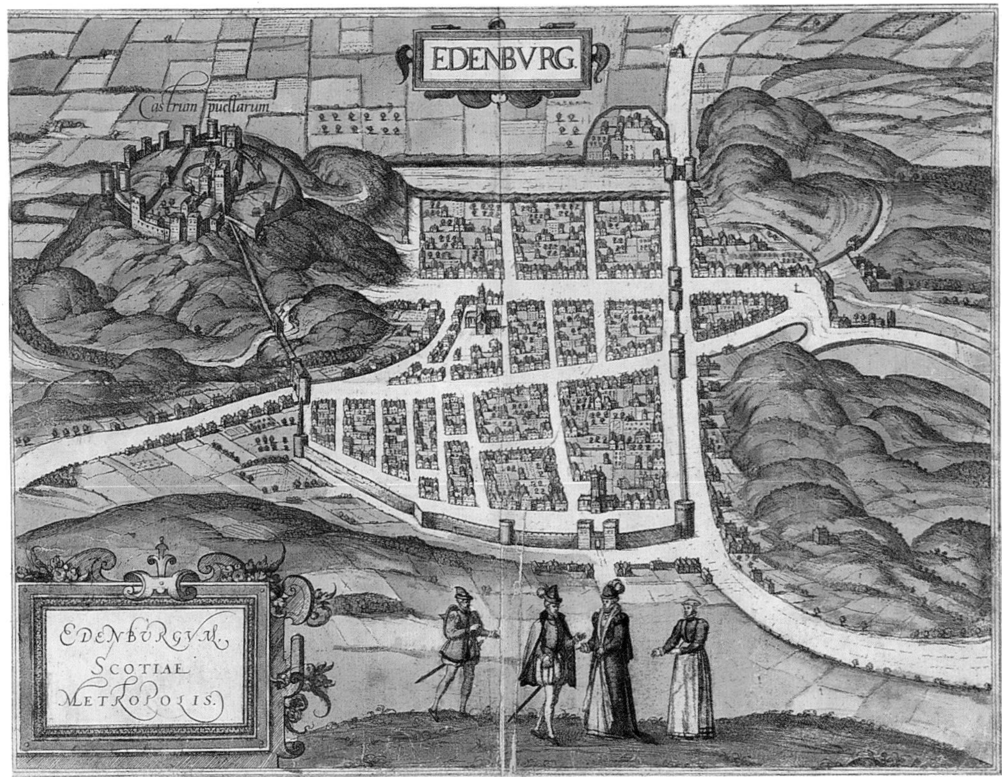

134. Plan of Edinburgh in about 1582.
(National Library of Scotland)

in healthy, airy countryside ideally suited to a convalescent. On the way there, though, Darnley suddenly had a fit of panic and announced that he could not possibly lodge at Craigmillar. Perhaps he feared what the Lords might do to him in the comparative isolation of the Castle while the Queen was in Edinburgh. He insisted that he would stay at Holyrood and nowhere else.

Patiently, Mary pointed out to him the reason why he could not go there, and in the end a compromise was reached. He would instead be installed in a house at Kirk o'Field, much nearer Holyrood. It was just inside the town walls, it had a pleasant garden and although it was small it could be furnished suitably for him. Messengers went ahead to warn the royal household about the change of plan, and supplies were sent up from the Palace.

On 1 February, the royal procession clattered into the square at Kirk o'Field, where the Old College of the University now stands. In those days there were small, gabled houses on three sides of the square, with a large, three-storey mansion on the fourth side. It belonged to the Hamilton family, and Archbishop Hamilton was using it as his residence. The dwelling prepared for Darnley was the more modest Old Provost's Lodging.

According to one of his servants, Darnley behaved in characteristic manner when he arrived by announcing that he wanted to occupy the Hamilton's house. He made a fuss when he was told that this was impossible, but he was finally taken into the Old Provost's Lodging. His bedchamber was on the first floor, a room hung with tapestries confiscated from the Huntly family after Corrichie. A black bed was erected for him and there was an imposing chair covered in purple velvet, two or three red velvet cushions and a little table with a green velvet cover, also from Huntly's castle.

Next to the bed was placed a large bath, because frequent bathing helped the healing process after smallpox, and it would be easy for his servants to lift him in and out of it. When it was not being used it needed a cover and so the Queen gave instructions that a door should be taken from its hinges and used as a lid. Darnley pronounced himself reasonably satisfied with these arrangements but he considered the bed to be too shabby and so one of his own was brought up from Holyrood: a magnificent piece of furniture which had belonged to Mary's mother and was hung with suitably regal embroidered violet curtains.

Underneath Darnley's chamber was a room with a yellow and green bed. The hall, also on the ground floor, was hung with more of the Huntly tapestries and the establishment was completed by a small sitting room called the cabinet, a wardrobe, a cellar and a kitchen, which was in a separate building. Darnley's valet and two other servants would lodge with him and look after him.

From the moment when he arrived in Edinburgh, he made rapid progress. This, he wrote to his father, was entirely due to the attentiveness of 'my love the Queen'. It seemed as though the clock had been turned back and they were enjoying once more the happy relationship they had shared at Stirling, before their marriage, when Darnley had been convalescing after measles.

Mary never did anything half-heartedly and, having finally decided to set aside her differences with her husband, she seemed to be trying her best to begin again. His recent brush with death had left him in a chastened frame of mind and she may have imagined that there was still hope that she could reclaim him from his evil ways and make something of him. The sight of his wan, disfigured face and his obvious reliance upon her appealed to her strong maternal instincts and she found herself once more encouraging and protecting him. She was genuinely kind to him, and when she saw his real fears for his own safety, she impetuously offered to sleep in the room below his. This had not been planned beforehand, and she had to send one of her women down to the Palace to fetch a fur rug for her bed. She spent the nights of the Wednesday and the Friday of that week at Kirk o'Field.

During the day, Darnley was never left on his own. The Queen and large numbers of courtiers crowded into his chamber to chat to him and play cards. Mary was working hard to achieve a reconciliation between the Lords and him, but beneath their surface friendliness the atmosphere was charged with envy and dislike. Lord Robert, Mary's half-brother, could eventually bear it no longer and he spoke to Darnley privately, warning him that unless he fled at once, 'it would cost him his life'. In a panic, Darnley repeated this to Mary, but when she questioned Lord Robert he denied having said any such thing, presumably for fear that the others

135. *Henry, Lord Darnley,* about 1566, by an unknown artist. (Scottish National Portrait Gallery)

would take reprisals against him.

Darnley was reassured, and by Sunday, 9 February, he was feeling so much better that it was agreed that he should move back to Holyrood the very next morning. That Sunday was a particularly busy one at Court, for one of the Queen's favourite pages, Bastien Pages, was to be married. Mary attended the wedding banquet at noon, then she moved on to a house in the Canongate where the Bishop of the Isles was giving a banquet for the departing ambassador of Savoy. Argyll, Huntly and Bothwell were among those present, resplendently clad in the masquing costumes they would wear for the continuing celebrations of Bastien's wedding that evening. The only person who was missing was the Earl of Moray. He had sent his apologies, explaining that he had just received word that his wife had suffered a miscarriage. He had to go to her.

After the Bishop's banquet was over, the Queen and her courtiers rode up to Kirk o'Field. Strolling into Darnley's chamber they laughed and joked, giving him their descriptions of the day's jollifications. Some of them sat down and played dice at the green covered table. They had been late in arriving, and everyone was tired now. The Queen meant to spend the night in the downstairs room, but between ten and eleven o'clock someone, Maitland of Lethington according to some accounts, reminded her about the wedding masque which would take place at the Palace. Mary had promised to attend, he claimed, and Bastien would be sadly disappointed if she did not put in an appearance. Mary hesitated. Darnley began to protest loudly that she had promised to stay with him, but her sense of duty to her own retinue was always strong and if Bastien expected her she could not disappoint him. After all, she and Darnley would be living together as man and wife from the very next day onwards.

She said she would go, and when her husband showed signs of having a tantrum, she patted him kindly and promised that she would make amends. He still was not mollified so she took one of the rings from her finger and gave it to him as a token of her affection, then she went downstairs. Emerging into the square, she came face to face with Paris, one of the royal attendants, who had formerly been employed by the Earl of Bothwell. His face was smeared with some kind of soot, and she exclaimed, 'Jesu, Paris! How begrimed you are!'

He said nothing, but she noticed that he got very red in the face. She stared at him for a moment, then she mounted her horse and rode with her courtiers back to Holyrood.

Behind her, at Kirk o'Field, Darnley called for some wine and made arrangements for his departure the next morning. He gave orders for his horses to be ready at the surprisingly early hour of five o'clock, which would be long before daylight. Often he enjoyed some music in the late evening but this time he did not call for his lute. Instead, he and one of his servants sang 'a merry song' together and then his valet, an English lad named Taylor, snuffed out the candles before retiring to his own mattress in the same room.

Down the hill at Holyrood, the Queen had arrived to find that the masque was almost over, but she was in time for the ceremonial bedding of bride and groom. When that was done, amidst the usual high-spirited teasing, she retired to her own chamber. She could not have been asleep for long when a deafening explosion seemed to shake the entire town. Waking with a start, she asked her ladies what cannon were firing, but no one knew. Amidst the alarm and confusion the Earl of Bothwell appeared. He had been sleeping in the Palace after the masque and he now began to rush about, making a great show of taking charge of the situation. After all, he was sheriff of Edinburgh and if there had been some disaster it was his business to investigate. Messengers were dispatched to find out what was happening.

Throughout the town, people had risen from their beds, pulled on their clothes and hurried outside. Those who lived near Kirk o'Field were greeted by a startling scene. The Old Provost's Lodging had been completely demolished. All that remained was a pile of rubble. Suddenly, the eerie silence was broken by hoarse cries for help. Men with lanterns hastened up and there, standing on the town wall which ran along behind the Lodging, they saw a tattered figure. It was Darnley's servant, Nelson.

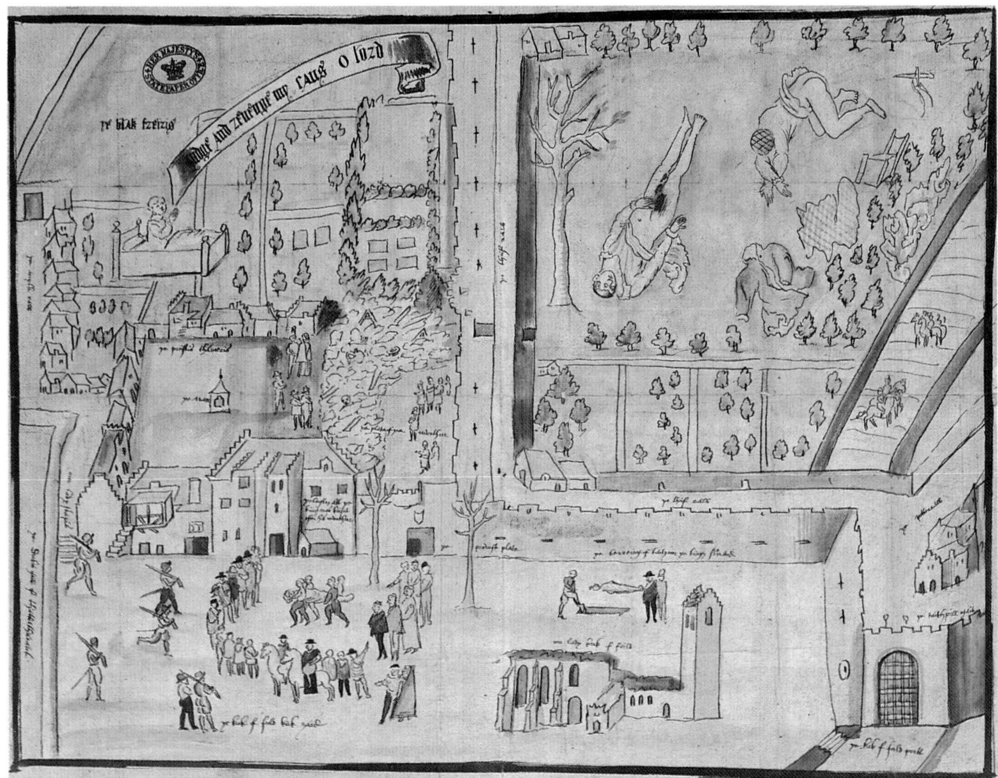

136. Drawing of the scene after the explosion at Kirk o' Field.
(Public Record Office, London)

Somehow or other, he had escaped the blast.

At the sight of him, the neighbours realised that there might be others buried in the ruins, and they began to dig about frantically among the fallen masonry. It was pitch dark, of course, and a bitterly cold night, with the occasional flurry of snow. Some time passed, perhaps half an hour, perhaps longer. The rescuers discovered first one body in the rubble and then another, but both corpses were identified as servants. Of Lord Darnley there was no sign. A considerable interval elapsed before someone happened to go into the garden beyond the town wall and there, away from all the activity, they came upon a macabre sight. Beneath a tree lay the body of the Queen's husband, clad only in his nightshirt. A yard or two away was the corpse of Taylor, the valet. Nearby were a chair, a dagger, a coat and a cloak. According to some eye witnesses, these belongings were laid down as neatly as though they had been placed there on purpose, although that is not the impression given by the drawing of the scene which was sent to Sir William Cecil in London.

Soon a large crowd gathered to peer at the unfortunate victims, and everyone gazed in wonderment. Neither Darnley nor the valet bore any signs of violence. There was no indication that they had been anywhere near the explosion. Their hair and their clothes were completely unsinged and unblackened by smoke, and the chair and the cloak were uncharred. Not a mark could be seen on the corpses: no dagger wounds, no sign of any gunshot wound, no indication of strangling or beating; nothing.

137. Account of expenses for Bastien Page's marriage and for the 'opening and perfuming' of Lord Darnley's body. (Scottish Record Office)

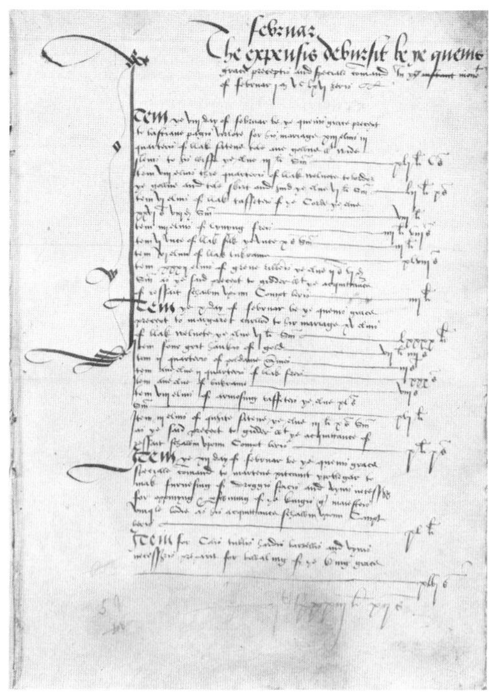

They carried Darnley's corpse into the house next to the demolished Lodging, and doctors were summoned to examine it, in the presence of some of the Lords of the Privy Council. After that, the general public were allowed to view the corpse, presumably to convince everyone that he was really dead. The body was then placed upon a board and carried unceremoniously down to the Palace.

It was the Earl of Bothwell who brought the news to the Queen that her husband had been killed, and she was completely stunned. The murderers, whoever they were, must have planned to kill her too. Of that she felt sure, for everyone had known that she was spending some of her nights at Kirk o'Field and but for her last minute change of plan she would have been there that very evening. They had planned to murder her, seize the baby Prince and rule the country for themselves, these evil Lords who had already murdered Riccio and threatened her own life at that time.

Bothwell told people next morning that the Queen was 'sorrowful and quiet', and she herself later described how she had been 'so grieved and tormented' at Darnley's death that she was unable to attend to any of her usual correspondence or do any business. She gave orders that his body was to be embalmed and that it would lie in state in the Chapel Royal, for he had been a King. While he was there, her nobles insisted that she go and look at the corpse. She stood and gazed at him for a long time, saying nothing and betraying no emotion. Usually, her feelings were near the surface and tears came readily, but now she could not weep.

The funeral took place towards the end of the week. Darnley was buried in James V's vault at Holyrood, by night. He was only twenty. So how had he really died? This question perturbed contemporaries and it has

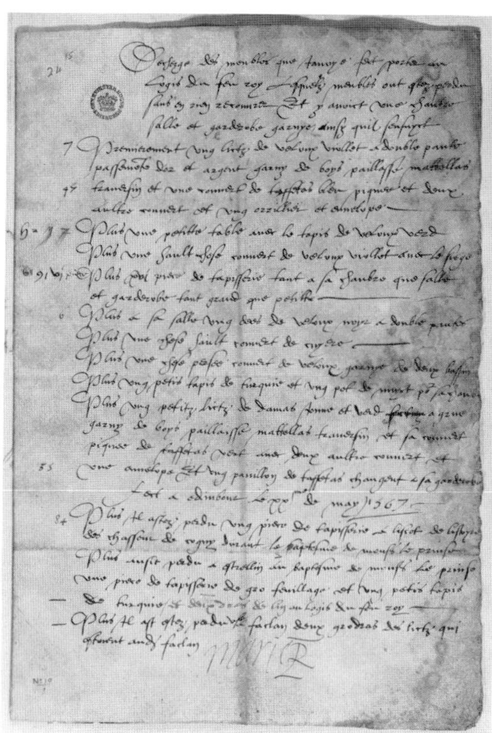

138. List, in French, of the royal furniture destroyed in the explosion at Kirk o' Field: the list begins with the velvet bed and the little table with the green cover. (Scottish Record Office)

tantalised writers ever since. The events of that strange night are shrouded in mystery. Statements by some of the minor men involved give us brief glimpses of the Earl of Bothwell hurrying to Kirk o'Field, his men lighting a fuse to set off gunpowder somehow smuggled into the house, and his own impatient and reckless expedition to see that the fuse was properly lit when ignition was in fact imminent. Some women who lived nearby told of hearing Darnley's voice raised in fear, his scream of 'Pity me, kinsmen, for the sake of Jesus Christ who pitied all the world . . .' then silence. Had he been intercepted trying to escape? Had he been asphyxiated in the garden by members of the Douglas family, perhaps, who were his own relatives? Mary always seemed to believe that he had died in the explosion, overcome by the smoke, but that was hardly possible, given the unmarked condition of his body. More important, was the whole tragic affair Bothwell's idea, or were others involved?

We shall probably never know the truth of it, but modern scholars incline to the view that many more people than Bothwell plotted the explosion. Indeed, it seems more or less certain that, at Craigmillar Castle the previous November, Maitland, Morton, Bothwell, probably Moray, and many more agreed that they would kill the husband of the Queen. Because his death would lay them open to charges of treason as well as of murder, they had to make sure that they were all equally implicated. Bothwell was doubtless responsible for introducing gunpowder into the house and laying the fuse, but he was acting in concert with many accomplices, and it is almost certain that it was Morton's followers who

139. Memorial painting of Henry, Lord Darnley, by L. de Vogeleer, painted in 1568 for his parents who are seen kneeling in the foreground, their son Charles behind them, the infant Prince James in front of them demanding vengeance. Inset is the scene at Carberry Hill. (Reproduced by gracious permission of Her Majesty The Queen)

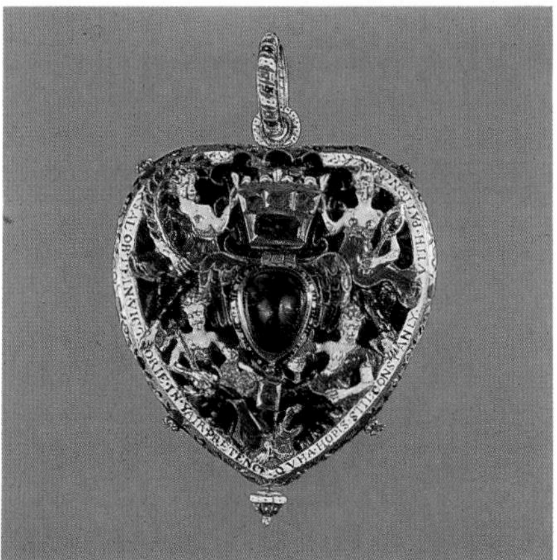

140. The Darnley Jewel, made for Darnley's mother in the 1570s, with complex emblems and inscriptions referring to her dead husband and her ambition that her murdered son's heir should one day be King of England. (Reproduced by gracious permission of Her Majesty The Queen)

slew the escaping Darnley. It is also fairly obvious that even had the Queen acted completely out of character and participated in the plan, she would have plotted something far more effective and far less crude than the blowing up of an entire building. Poison in a cup of wine would have been much easier to arrange and would not have involved the uncertainties of the Kirk o'Field scheme.

It is much more plausible that she knew nothing, that the Lords successfully concealed their purpose from her just as they had done before the Riccio killing. It is also likely that some of them were aiming at her death as well. That did not apply to Bothwell, of course, for his ambitions were rather different. In the hours after Darnley's murder, he strove hard to convince her of his own innocence and in this he succeeded. Amidst the violence, the treachery and the bloodshed, Mary turned to him gladly, believing him to be completely reliable and utterly devoted to the crown.

141. *James, Earl of Bothwell,* and his first wife, *Lady Jean Gordon,* by an unknown artist.
(Scottish National Portrait Gallery)

142. The coat of arms of James, Earl of Bothwell, from the Forman Armorial.
(National Library of Scotland)

8
THE EARL OF BOTHWELL

FOR FORTY days after the tragedy at Kirk o'Field, the Queen was expected to observe formal mourning and remain in her chamber, cut off from the outside world. However, by the end of the first week her doctors had decided that there were 'great and imminent dangers to her health and life if she did not in all speed break up and leave that kind of close, solitary life and repair to some good, wholesome air'. Accordingly, she went along the coast to Lord Seton's house, leaving her baby son in the care of Bothwell and his brother-in-law, the Earl of Huntly.

Her choice of guardians did not go unnoticed, and the day after she left town a placard appeared on the door of the Tolbooth. Its message was simple and direct. Bothwell had murdered Darnley. During the next few nights more notices appeared, some illustrated with crude protraits of the Earl and all bearing the same accusation. When he saw them, Bothwell reacted in typical fashion. He flew into a fury, vowed vengeance on those responsible and voiced the intention of washing his hands in their blood.

In spite of his threats, the notices continued and now they bore a much more sinister legend, for they claimed that the Queen had known of the murder in advance. On 1 March a new theme was depicted. A drawing appeared showing a hare surrounded by a circle of swords and accompanied by a sketch of a crowned mermaid. The meaning was plain to all who saw it. Accustomed to symbols and emblems, people at once recognised that the hare was the animal on Bothwell's family crest. A mermaid was the popular way of representing a prostitute and as this mermaid wore a crown there was no doubting her identity. From then onwards there was a growing storm of rumour to the effect that the Queen and her lover had murdered her unfortunate husband.

When she was told about the accusations, the Queen's reaction was not one of guilt but of indignation. The very man who had stood by her through all her troubles was now being attacked by the real murderers, and she hastened to his defence. She was seen with him in public, she consulted him about affairs of state and she gave him a series of valuable gifts. Her friends were horrified, for if she could not see where her actions were leading, they certainly could. If she associated with him, she would lay herself open to charges of having been involved in the murder too, yet even with these warnings she was fatally slow in taking action. Despite the urgings of her father-in-law, the Earl of Lennox, she failed to prosecute those responsible for her husband's murder. Instead of arraigning them before parliament, she left it to Lennox to accuse the guilty Lords and he at once named Bothwell.

His trial was fixed for 12 April and he was one of the Privy Councillors who made the arrangements for it. Full of righteous indignation, Lennox marched from the west with a body of three thousand men. When he reached Linlithgow he was told he must leave his army at home and

143. Crichton Castle, one of Bothwell's strongholds. (Historic Buildings and Monuments, SDD)

appear in the capital with no more than six companions. Since Bothwell had filled Edinburgh with his own men, it was more than Lennox's life was worth to come unprotected, and he turned round and went home.

On the morning of 12 April, Bothwell mounted his horse in the forecourt of Holyrood, then he looked up to the Queen's window and waved his hand. She acknowledged his greeting with a friendly nod. Satisfied, he set off on the short ride up the Canongate to the Tolbooth, accompanied by more than four thousand men. Proceedings lasted throughout the day. For more than eight hours, the Court listened to evidence, but in the absence of both the Queen and Lennox there was no one to accuse the Earl and so he was acquitted. Four days later he was back at the Tolbooth again, but under very different circumstances. This time, the Queen was opening parliament and the man who paced along in the royal procession bearing the sceptre was none other than the Earl of Bothwell. During the deliberations which followed, she formally took the Reformed Church under the protection.

Those hostile to Mary have seen in this strange sequence of events the final evidence of her guilt, while her defenders have pleaded that, overwhelmed by the traumatic events of the previous twelve months, she lost control of the situation completely and could not be held responsible for her actions. She was either suffering from a nervous collapse, or the hereditary disease, porphyria, and so she could not be blamed for anything she did.

Neither of these explanations rings true. Mary turned to Bothwell because he was a strong man, she thought, and she believed that by taking him as her principal adviser she would give her decisions a masculine authority which her other Lords would be forced to respect. She was to describe him later as 'a man of resolution, well adapted to rule' and that exactly sums up his principal attraction for her. She was interested above all else in the exercise of power and she was determined to go on governing the country somehow or other.

Mary therefore intended to associate Bothwell in government with her. He certainly was not high-born enough to enter her calculations as a possible husband and she had no need of him as a consort. He would serve her as a faithful subject committed to her interests. The Earl, of course, had other ideas. With his past history of profligacy he was well accustomed to using women for his own purposes and now, observing Mary's friendliness towards him, he decided that the highest place in the realm was within his grasp. He would divorce his wife and marry the Queen instead.

That spring, he proposed to her on several occasions, and each time she refused him. He decided to pursue his campaign from a different direction and, when parliament closed after only three days of debate, he invited a group of those who had attended to take supper with him after the final session. They met, probably in Ainslie's Tavern, and by a combination of threats and promises he persuaded them to sign an agreement saying that he was innocent of any complicity in Darnley's murder and declaring that they would recommend him as a husband to the Queen.

Mary knew that if she accepted his proposal she would run the risk of ruining herself forever, for everyone would then believe that she had been guilty of complicity in Darnley's death, yet now eight bishops, ten earls and eleven lords were urging her to take the very course of action which most appealed to her. The fact that Bothwell already had a wife hardly seemed to matter to anyone, least of all Lady Jean herself, who seems to have given some clear indication that she was willing to release him. Even so, Mary hesitated. The Earl, after all, was only an Earl. He was far beneath her in status and, unlike Darnley, he had no royal blood. She hesitated, and as she did so more letters from her friends abroad arrived, warning her of the dire consequences of entering into the marriage.

To Mary's mind she was not contemplating marrying a murderer: she was thinking of taking as her husband a man whom rumour had falsely accused of a terrible crime and if she was to go ahead it would need to be in such a way that the match seemed to have been forced upon her, without her own volition. She had lengthy talks with the ingenious Maitland of Lethington, while Bothwell was growing visibly impatient, and towards the end of April the period of uncertainty ended.

On the 20th of that month, the Queen decided to go to Stirling to visit her son. She spent a few days with him, then she set out for Edinburgh again, travelling with an entourage of about thirty people, including Huntly, Maitland and Sir James Melville. They spent a night at Linlithgow on the way home and then, about six miles from Edinburgh, suddenly they saw a small army bearing down upon them with the Earl of Bothwell at its head.

He rode straight up to the Queen, placed his hand on her bridle and told her that there was danger in the capital and he was taking her to Dunbar Castle for safety. Some of her party objected but she silenced them. There was to be no more bloodshed, she said. She would go with the Earl. Most of her entourage were allowed to go on their way but she, Huntly, Maitland and Melville were escorted to Dunbar. Bothwell had sworn to marry her whether she agreed or not, and now, according to Sir James, he 'ravished her' and lay with her against her will.

When, towards the end of her life, she reminisced about her career to Nau, her French secretary, she never did go into details about the Dunbar episode. In some ways this was not surprising but, had she really been taken against her will, Mary was far more likely to have been full of wrathful condemnation of the man involved. As it was, she never uttered any real criticism of Bothwell and she told the Bishop of Dunblane shortly after her alleged abduction that, with regard to Bothwell, 'Albeit we found his doings rude, yet were his answer and words but gentle'. The most likely explanation of events is that the Queen had agreed to some form of 'abduction' but that she intended it as a preliminary to betrothal and marriage. Bothwell, determined that she would not change her mind, insisted on having intercourse with her there and then.

After that, she had no choice but to make firm plans to take him as her husband. Two days after Mary was taken to Dunbar, Lady Bothwell began proceedings for a Protestant divorce, alleging that her husband had committed adultery with one of her servants. The day after that, Bothwell applied for an annulment. Lady Bothwell was granted her divorce on 3 May. Five days later, Bothwell got his annulment. In the eyes of both his Church and Mary's he was free to marry.

On 6 May they returned to Edinburgh. The Queen rode in procession through the West Port with the Castle guns firing in salute and Bothwell by her side. The crowds were quick to notice that he led her horse by the bridle, as if she were his prisoner. That same day, one of the Edinburgh ministers was asked to proclaim the banns for a Protestant marriage between the Queen and the Earl. He refused to do so, because he believed that she was being forced into the match against her will, but on the following day the Lord Justice Clerk brought him a document signed by the Queen saying that she had neither been kept captive nor raped. Later that week, she made Bothwell Duke of Orkney, placing his coronet upon his head with her own hands. She also appeared before the assembled judges and announced that she had forgiven him for abducting her and would now marry him.

The marriage contract was signed on 14 May, with Huntly and Maitland appearing among the witnesses to it. On 15 May the wedding took place. May marriages were very unpopular in Scotland, usually avoided at all

144. *John Leslie, Bishop of Ross,* to whom Mary confided her regrets after her Protestant marriage to Bothwell; portrait by an unknown artist. (Scottish National Portrait Gallery)

costs, but this was a far from normal occasion. It took place at ten o'clock in the morning, according to the Protestant rite. The service was conducted by Bothwell's friend, the Bishop of Orkney, and it was held in the Great Hall at Holyrood, where the Privy Council usually met.

Once more, as at her marriage to Darnley, the Queen was in deepest mourning. Her husband, after all, had been dead for just over three months and so there was no light-hearted ceremony of changing widow's weeds for garments of gaiety. There was no rejoicing at all, in fact, no masques and no dancing. Instead, the Queen and her new husband sat down to dinner at opposite ends of the table in an atmosphere of gloom. Outside, someone had put up a placard bearing in Latin the quotation which translates as, 'Wantons marry in the month of May'.

The French ambassador, who was one of the guests, thought he detected a strange formality between the newly wed couple and he remarked upon it. The Queen brushed his comments aside, merely saying somewhat curtly that it was a solemn occasion. That afternoon, when she saw Bishop Leslie, she burst into tears and, sobbing bitterly, assured him that she would never abandon the Catholic Church and that she already regretted marrying according to the Protestant form. She promised him vehemently that she would never do anything to harm what he and she

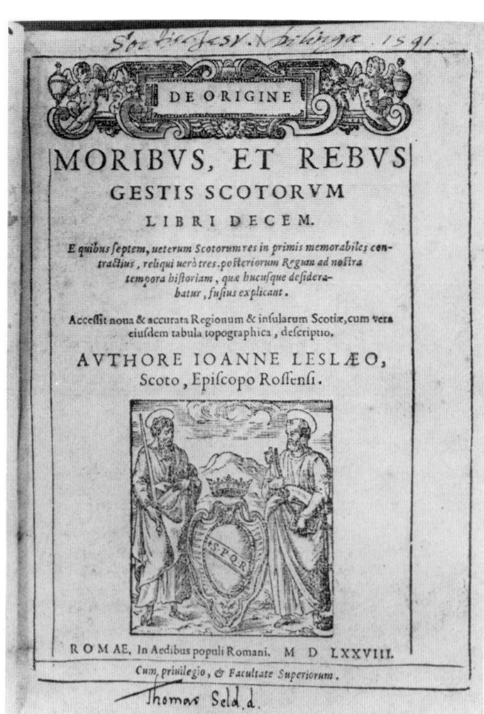

DE ORIGINE

MORIBVS, ET REBVS

GESTIS SCOTORVM

LIBRI DECEM.

E quibus septem, ueterum Scotorum res in primis memorabiles contractius, reliqui uerò tres posteriorum Regum ad nostra tempora historiam, quæ hucusque desiderabatur, fusius explicant.

Accessit noua & accurata Regionum & insularum Scotiæ, cum vera eiusdem tabula topographica, descriptio.

AVTHORE IOANNE LESLÆO, Scoto, Episcopo Rossensi.

ROMAE, In Aedibus populi Romani. M D LXXVIII.

Cum priuilegio, & Facultate Superiorum.

145. Title page of one of the histories written by the Bishop of Ross, who defended Mary. (National Library of Scotland)

knew to be the true religion and the following Sunday she apparently attended public communion.

Mary had made this marriage for largely political reasons but, as soon as Bothwell was actually her husband, she realised that she had betrayed her own standards and her own deeper feelings. If, as her enemies suggested, she had married for sexual satisfaction, she should have been delighted at being united with the man she loved. As it was, the situation was entirely different. She had thought that she could put personal happiness aside in the pursuit of power but, while her first two marriages had brought her difficulties, neither had required her to abandon her religion or lower her own status. She soon discovered that relying on Bothwell as a friend was very different from being his wife. He had no notion of how to behave as her consort, and from the beginning she suffered from the dreadful knowledge that she had dishonoured herself and ruined her reputation by taking him as her husband.

When other people were present, he treated her with almost exaggerated respect, going bareheaded when he alone now had the right to wear a hat in her presence. She was seen to look at him reprovingly on those occasions, and sometimes she would take his bonnet out of his hands and place it on his head for him. If he was overly deferential in public, he was far too familiar in private, doing nothing to moderate his rumbustious behaviour in her presence and embarrassing her with his lack of finesse. He never did learn how to be polite for diplomatic reasons, she once remarked sadly, and there was little hope that she could change his ways. Even Darnley had had the advantage that he was young and malleable: Bothwell was too mature and too opinionated to alter his behaviour for anyone.

The Lords, of course, were beside themselves with jealousy and rage when they realised that he was really going to become the Queen's husband and that he would now treat them as though he were their monarch. They were ready to pounce upon and exaggerate every little sign that he and Mary might be quarrelling, and they gladly passed round stories of her weeping and declaring that she wanted to kill herself. The foreign ambassadors who saw husband and wife together were prophesying that this marriage would never last, but the courtiers had no intention of waiting for the inevitable divorce and, before the wedding had even taken place, they were plotting Bothwell's downfall.

On 1 May they had met at Stirling to draw up a new bond, promising this time to free Mary from the Earl. To this end, they gathered together an army and marched towards Borthwick Castle, where the Queen and her husband had gone soon after their wedding. Having no adequate means of defending themselves, Mary and Bothwell made hasty plans for escape. No doubt it was she who thought up this latest scheme to elude her enemies, for he was more likely to rush out in a fury to encounter the opposition, regardless of the consequences. The castle was not heavily defended and it would not have withstood a siege, so they agreed to talk to the Lords. While Mary spoke to them, declining their offer to escort her back to Edinburgh, Bothwell slipped out of the Castle unnoticed and disappeared. Next morning the Queen put on men's clothing, made her way to the castle gates and rode off to meet her husband at a prearranged rendezvous. From there they rode to the much safer Dunbar Castle.

Raising an army of their own had become a matter of urgency, and the next few days were spent summoning their followers, particularly from the Border area. By mid-June they were ready, and at the head of a force roughly equal in size to that of the Lords, they rode towards Edinburgh. On 15 June, exactly a month after the wedding, the two armies met at Carberry, near Musselburgh.

Mary was in a mood of angry resentment that day and she took the field vowing vengeance on her rebellious Lords. She and her army marched up to a position on Carberry Hill, facing the enemy who were drawn up on another hill opposite with Morton, Lindsay, Ruthven and Kirkcaldy of Grange as their leaders. Above the Lords fluttered a huge white banner upon which was painted the body of Darnley lying beneath his tree. In front of him knelt Prince James, with the words 'Judge and avenge my cause, O Lord' inscribed above his head.

It was almost midsummer and the day was hot, with the sun beating down. As the armies faced each other, unmoving, a small figure on horseback came into view, riding towards the Queen. It was the French ambassador, who had been persuaded to act as intermediary. The message he gave Mary was that if she would abandon Bothwell, the Lords would restore her to her rightful position. She received this offer with indignation. These were the very men who had urged her to marry the Earl in the first place, she exclaimed, and she had no intention of deserting him because they had changed their minds. The ambassador departed with her reply.

146. Contemporary drawing of the scene at Carberry Hill, with Mary on horseback being led by Kirkcaldy of Grange from her own army towards the rebel Lords. (Public Record Office, London)

The two forces, evenly matched, continued to survey each other from a distance until the Lords, perhaps playing for time, came up with a new suggestion. The whole issue could be settled in single combat, they said. This idea appealed to Bothwell, of course. Over-confident, rash as ever and excited he made to spur his horse forward but the Queen stopped him. If he were killed she would lose her general and her army would be in disarray. Slowly the day dragged on. Further challenges for personal combat were made and declined, then at last Kirkcaldy of Grange appeared and repeated the Lords' offer. If Mary put away her husband, they would give her their loyalty.

By now, it was almost evening and everyone was exhausted with the heat, lack of food and the strain of waiting. The Queen looked round about and she realised that her army was beginning to drift away. All her hopes of a decisive victory had gone, and her position was desperate. To add to her troubles and her feeling of malaise, she was, whether she knew it or not, in the early weeks of pregnancy with Bothwell's child. He was about to take up Lord Lindsay's challenge to fight, so before he risked his life she decided that she must take the only honourable way out. She told Kirkcaldy that she agreed to the Lords' proposition. If they kept their word and restored her to her proper place, she would send Bothwell away and come to them herself.

Her husband was reluctant to go, but she persuaded him that if they wanted to save themselves he must obey her. He should stay away until parliament could meet and investigate the murder of Darnley. Then, she

147. The design on the banner carried by the Lords at Carberry Hill. (Public Record Office, London)

said, if he were proved innocent, 'nothing would prevent her from rendering to him all that a true and lawful wife ought to do,' but if he were found guilty, 'it would be to her an endless source of regret that, by their marriage, she had ruined her good reputation, and from this she would endeavour to free herself by every possible means.'

Finally, he agreed. Before he went, he produced a bond signed by Morton, Lethington and the others agreeing to murder Darnley. He solemnly swore to her that anything he himself had done had been entirely on their advice and by their persuasions. She should keep it safely, he said, and then he rode off.

As he did so, Kirkcaldy of Grange approached the Queen and she said to him,

'Laird of Grange, I render myself unto you, upon the conditions you rehearsed unto me, in the name of the Lords.'

She gave him her hand to kiss, then he took her horse by its bridle and led her down the slope towards the enemy camp. Hot and dishevelled, she advanced proudly towards what she took to be an honourable reception, her domestic servants following behind her, but almost at once she was rudely disillusioned. Instead of cheering her or even waiting in respectful silence, the soldiers began to hurl coarse insults at her, nor was the bearing of the Lords themselves reassuring. Their grim expressions hardly promised friendship or a return to obedience. Seeing the Earl of Morton among them, the Queen exclaimed sharply,

'How is this, My Lord Morton? I am told that all this is done in order to get justice among the King's murderers. I am also told that you are one of the chief of them!'

'Come, come,' he retorted, 'This is not the place to discuss such matters,' and then he slunk away. The shouting and the abuse continued. 'Burn the whore!' the soldiers yelled, until Grange and one or two of his friends, ashamed, drew their swords and threatened their own men if they did not keep quiet. An uneasy silence fell, and in an atmosphere of brooding tension they set out for Edinburgh.

Two particularly harsh and intimidating young men had been chosen to ride by the Queen, and when at last they all entered the town gates she was separated from her servants and surrounded by soldiers. In that moment, she realised that she was a prisoner. Her hair had come unpinned and hung down in tangled strands, her red petticoat was filthy with dust and her face was streaked with tears. As soon as her cavalcade entered the capital, they were almost deafened by the jeering of the crowd. Men, women and children thronged every outside stair, hung out of every window, screaming and shouting the crudest of insults and everywhere there were cries of 'Kill her! Drown her!'

She had thought that they would take her to Holyrood, but instead they came to a halt outside the Provost of Edinburgh's house. She was curtly ordered to dismount and shown inside. There, she found those Lords who had ridden ahead preparing to sit down to supper. They asked her to join them, but she answered that they had already provided her with supper enough, considering the condition to which she saw herself reduced. She needed rest more than food.

At that, they shut her up in a sparsely furnished bedchamber which, even in her state of exhaustion, she noted as being entirely unsuitable for a Queen. Guards were posted at the doors and on the stairs, and some of the soldiers remained in the room with her. This meant that she could not undress and go to bed. Even in that extremity, she managed to persuade the soldiers to allow her to write one or two letters and somehow she sent a message to the captain of Edinburgh Castle urging him to keep a 'good heart' towards her and hold the stronghold against the Lords. Only after that did she lie down, clothed, on the bed for an hour or two.

Next morning when she got up and looked out of the window, the first object to meet her gaze was the white banner with the body of Darnley under the tree. The Lords had brought it with them from Carberry and hung it up opposite so that she could not avoid seeing it. Later, about eight or nine o'clock, she noticed Maitland of Lethington coming towards her lodging. Frantically she called his name and, weeping, she reminded him of all her past kindness to him. She begged him to come and speak to her, but he pulled his hat down over his eyes and pretended not to see her.

A crowd had gathered outside the house, and even the most hostile were shocked at the sight of their Queen, once so elegant and so charming, with her long hair hanging down over her shoulders, her chemise half torn open and her face haggard and white. She had been betrayed, she shrieked desperately, and she was being kept prisoner. Before she could say any more, guards came and pulled her away from the window, telling her that for her own safety she must not look out again.

148. Monument at the site of Carberry Hill. (Photograph, Michael Brooks)

Meanwhile, the Lords were making their plans. Kirkcaldy and some of the others would have been satisfied with having separated Mary from Bothwell but the others had more wide-ranging ambitions. Morton and his friends were determined to seize power and they also knew that Mary could give damning testimony of their part in Darnley's murder. She must be taken away from Edinburgh to some isolated place and there they could deal with her once and for all. Kirkcaldy refused to agree, for he had given her his word that she would be restored, but Morton and the others now produced a letter which they said Mary had written to Bothwell the previous night. Addressing him as 'dear heart' she apparently swore that she would never abandon him. This letter has never been found and there are grave doubts about whether it was genuine. Contemporaries said it was a forgery and Kirkcaldy refused to believe that the Queen had written it, but the Lords were determined. It was proof, they claimed, that she had already broken her part of the bargain. Kirkcaldy did not know what to say and his companions quickly pressed on with their plans.

That evening, the Queen had a brief visit from Maitland. She demanded a parliamentary enquiry into Darnley's death, saying that this would vindicate her. He refused and warned her that the Council would never allow her to take Bothwell back. In spite of his bold words, though, she noticed that not once did he raise his eyes and look her in the face.

He went away and about nine o'clock the Earl of Morton appeared at her door and ordered her to get ready to leave. They were taking her to Holyrood. Her hopes were raised, and when they reached the Palace she

149. *George Buchanan*, one of the principal accusers of Mary, by an unknown artist.
(Scottish National Portrait Gallery)

was reunited with the members of her household, including Mary Seton and Mary Livingston. Since the morning of Carberry Hill the Queen had scarcely eaten anything. Fearful of being poisoned, she had drunk only water and taken a little bread. Now, she allowed her ladies to persuade her to sit down to supper and she ate, even though Morton was standing impatiently behind her chair all the time.

Suddenly, in the middle of the meal, he asked one of the servants if the

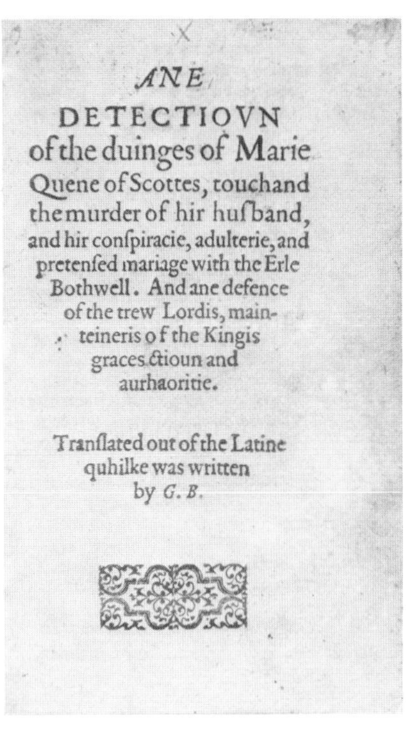

ANE
DETECTIOVN
of the duinges of Marie
Quene of Scottes, touchand
the murder of hir huſband,
and hir conſpiracie, adulterie, and
pretenſed mariage with the Erle
Bothwell. And ane defence
of the trew Lordis, main-
teineris of the Kingis
graces actioun and
aurhaoritie.

Tranſlated out of the Latine
quhilke was written
by *G. B.*

150. Title page of one of Buchanan's books claiming to prove Mary's guilt: the original was in Latin.

horses were ready, ordered the plates to be taken away and told the Queen to prepare for a ride. Bewildered, she asked where they were going and he gave her to understand that they would visit her son at Stirling. Despite the pleas and tears of her servants, only two chamber women were allowed to go with her and she was not allowed to take any extra clothing except a nightdress.

With Lord Ruthven, the son of Riccio's murderer, on one side and Lord Lindsay on the other, she was taken down to Leith in the gathering gloom. On the way, someone got word to her that the Hamiltons would try to rescue her, and she tried to fall behind. Ruthven and Lindsay noticed, however, and they whipped her horse on. As they rode northwards towards Kinross, she saw that she was not going to see Prince James at all, and she realised that captivity lay ahead.

151. Lochleven Castle, viewed from the loch. (Historic Buildings and Monuments, SDD)

9

LOCHLEVEN

LATE AT night they arrived at Lochleven, where the Earl of Moray's half-brother, Sir William Douglas, had a castle. The Queen was rowed hastily across the lake to this stronghold and ushered unceremoniously into the apartment normally occupied by Sir William himself. The Earl of Morton signed a warrant authorising her imprisonment and the next morning he and the others departed for Edinburgh, leaving Lord Ruthven and Lord Lindsay in charge of her.

Distraught, sick and furious, Mary refused to eat, drink or even talk to her captors. By the end of a fortnight she was seriously ill, and she recognised the fact that nothing she did would change the Lords' attitude towards her. If she were to survive, she would have to come to terms with her imprisonment. She began to take nourishment and after a month there were reports that she 'better digests' her captivity. In mid-July, one of the English envoys was told that she was 'calmed and better quieted than of late, and takes both rest and meat, and also some dancing and play at the cards, much better than she was wont to do and, so as it is said, she is become fat'.

The Lords were anxious to reassure their friends in the south, for the English had shown an unexpected degree of agitation about the Queen's captivity. Elizabeth expressed horror at any monarch being treated in such a fashion and she dispatched Sir Nicholas Throckmorton north on what he was soon describing as the most dangerous mission of his career. All his attempts to see Mary failed and he reported that she was in deadly peril. The best he could do was to smuggle messages to her warning of 'the great rage and fury of the people against her' and beseeching her to save herself by divorcing Bothwell. Her reply gave him no comfort. She would rather die, she said, that do that, for 'taking herself to be seven weeks gone with child, she should acknowledge herself to be with child of a bastard and to have forfeited her honour' if she made a move to end the marriage.

Throckmorton despaired. If she continued on this course, the Lords would surely make away with her, he believed. They were deaf to all Elizabeth's threats and it would be all too easy for them to arrange for Mary to drown in the waters of the loch one night. They had only to say that she had killed herself or that she had died trying to escape and no more questions would be asked. To make matters worse, he learned that the Lords were now demanding that she should abdicate, and that she was refusing. This was a moment of crisis. He managed to smuggle another message in to her, hidden in the scabbard of the sword belonging to Sir James Melville's brother. In it, he urged her to agree in order to save her life. She could safely do that, for an abdication extorted by force was illegal and it could be set aside as soon as she was free once more.

Even then, the Queen still proudly refused, but events were about to force her hand. Some time around 23 July she suffered a miscarriage,

152. Lochleven Castle, general view. (Historic Buildings and Monuments, SDD)

doubtless brought on by stress, and it was found that she had parted with twins. Historians have argued ever since about the age of these babies, for Mary's accusers would like to believe that they were conceived during an adulterous affair with Bothwell even before Darnley met his death. In practical terms, this seems too unlikely to have been possible. If the infants were the fruit of a relationship in January, say, they would have been six months old at the time of the miscarriage and no Queen could have concealed a pregnancy for so long, least of all a twin pregnancy.

Even in normal circumstances the people around a female monarch were always alert for the slightest sign that a child was expected and, in Mary's case, the Earl of Moray's mother and Sir William Douglas' wife were constantly with her and they would certainly not have been deceived. Apart from anything else, if the twins had dated from before Darnley's death, Mary could have tried to pass them off as being his.

Mary's Dominican confessor solemnly swore to the Spanish ambassador in London that until the prospect of her marriage to Bothwell became an issue, he had never seen a woman of greater virtue, courage and uprightness, and he insisted that she had been completely innocent of Darnley's murder. There is certainly no evidence that she was unfaithful to him and so it seems acceptable that the twins were conceived after his death.

It is unlikely, though, that they dated from the time of her marriage to

153. *Sir Nicholas Throckmorton*, Queen Elizabeth's envoy, by an unknown artist, about 1562.
(National Portrait Gallery, London)

Bothwell, as she wanted to believe. If that had been so, the foetuses would only have been nine or ten weeks old at the time of the miscarriage. In other words, they would have measured no more than an inch long and would have been difficult to identify. It is much more probable that they were conceived at the time of the abduction to Dunbar, but the Queen did not necessarily tell deliberate lies about this. Women had no means of accurately determining the start of a pregnancy and mistakes in calculation were very frequent.

Whether the babies were nine or eleven weeks old scarcely mattered. What was important was the advantage their arrival gave to the Queen's enemies at the time. As soon as he heard that she was ill, Lord Lindsay arrived at her chamber to find her lying on her bed, very weak after losing a good deal of blood. Instead of feeling pity for her, he recognised this as the ideal moment to press the Lords' demands, and in a brutally menacing manner he demanded that she sign a document agreeing to abdicate. At such a low ebb, physically, she feared from his demeanour that he was about to kill her then and there. Remembering Throckmorton's advice that no signature extorted under such conditions could be deemed legal, she set aside her pride and told him that she would do as he asked.

He produced three papers. By the first, she resigned her crown to Prince James on the grounds that she was 'so vexed, broken and unquieted' by the toil of governing the country that she could no longer go on. The

154. The Church of the Holy Rude, Stirling, where Prince James was crowned. (Photograph, Michael Brooks)

second document named the Earl of Moray as Regent, and, as he was abroad, the third arranged for Morton and his associates to rule until he returned.

The Queen refused contemptuously to read the papers, but she did sign them, saying over and over again to those present that she would not be bound by their contents. The date was 24 July. Five days later, Prince James, now thirteen months old, was crowned at Stirling in the Protestant church beside the Castle. John Knox preached the sermon and Morton and Lord Home took the oath on behalf of the infant King. The guns of Edinburgh Castle fired a salute and at Lochleven Sir William Douglas sang and danced in his garden though he refused to tell the Queen what he was celebrating. Only the Hamilton family were excluded from the coronation and the rejoicings, a fact which they would not forget.

Immediately after her abdication, the Queen suffered a serious relapse, and when she recovered she was moved into the old, medieval tower of the castle, for greater security, she was told. It was also because she was becoming dangerously friendly with the members of Sir William's household. In other respects, her conditions improved slightly. After her abdication, she was allowed clothing from her wardrobe at Holyrood, and sewing materials. She was permitted to walk in the Castle gardens and indoors she played cards and even began to dance again.

In August, she received a visit from the Earl of Moray. When he had heard that he was to be Regent, he had been 'right glad' and, although he put on a suitable show of reluctance, it was of short duration. He hurried home to Scotland and four days after his return he arrived at Lochleven in company with Morton and other friends. Declining the Queen's invitation to take supper with her, he embarked nonetheless on a long

155. *James, Earl of Moray,* in later life, by an unknown artist. (The Duke of Hamilton, at Holyrood)

discussion with her after the meal, strolling in the garden and then sitting up late in her chamber. The interview was a stormy one. Having upbraided her for her folly in marrying Bothwell, he broached the subject of the regency and instead of telling her that he had accepted the position, he merely said that it had been offered to him, and asked her advice about accepting.

The Queen's reaction was swift and wrathful. If her Lords would not obey her, their rightful sovereign, how could he expect them to take orders from him, a King's bastard, she enquired, and she quoted an old saying: 'He who does not keep faith where it is due will hardly keep it where it is not due'. His suggestion that he would do her less harm as Regent than anyone else was not well received and when he went on to announce that in fact he had already accepted the position, Mary's anger knew no bounds. He went back to Edinburgh the next day, announcing that she

156. Book belonging to James, Earl of Moray, with his crest on the back cover. (National Library of Scotland)

had given him her approval, and within a week he was publicly proclaimed Regent. At once he took possession of her priceless jewels, many of which were her own private property, given to her by Francis II and his father. He presented some to his wife and the rest he prepared to sell.

While all this was taking place, the Earl of Bothwell made his escape from Scotland. After Carberry Hill he fled south to the Borders, where he passed some weeks trying energetically to raise more men for the royal cause. He then fled northwards to seek shelter with an aged relative, the Bishop of Moray, but, when the Bishop's illegitimate sons tried to murder him, he decided that the time had come to leave Scotland altogether. Fitting out five ships, he sailed first to Orkney and then on to Norway, where he had the bad luck to run into a group of his creditors and the resentful relatives of one of his cast-off mistresses. He was arrested and he passed the last eleven years of his life in a series of prisons, in horrifying conditions. His final days were spent in Dragsholm Castle in Denmark, where he was chained to a pillar half his height so that he could never stand upright. He died insane in 1578.

No longer tied to him by pregnancy, the Queen ceased to take account of him in her plans and she gave all her attention to her own immediate circumstances. At the beginning of December she would celebrate her twenty-fifth birthday, and the eve of this official coming of age was the traditional time for the Scottish monarch to take back any gifts of land which had been granted during his or her minority. Morton and many others were liable to lose valuable property as a result, and they were

157. List of clothes sent to Mary at Lochleven. (Scottish Record Office)

determined that she would never again have the opportunity to exercise power in Scotland.

When Mary heard that a parliament would be held that same month, she wrote a long letter to Moray demanding to be allowed to appear and clear herself of the charges against her as the Lords had promised at Carberry Hill that she should do. Moray's refusal was curt and dismissive. She could not appear. Instead of hearing an address from their sovereign, those who attended confirmed her abdication and Moray's appointment as Regent, and they went on to accuse her of having been 'privy, art and part' to the slaughter of Darnley. Hitherto the Lords had only condemned her for marrying Bothwell. Now they were saying that she was guilty as he of the murder at Kirk o'Field.

When she learned what had been said, the Queen redoubled her efforts to gain her freedom. 'It is by force alone that I can be delivered', she wrote to Catherine de Medici. 'If you send never so few troops to countenance the matter, I am certain great numbers of my subjects will rise to join them, but without that they are overawed by the power of the rebels and dare attempt nothing of themselves.'

She wrote not only to France but to England as well, complaining bitterly to Elizabeth that Moray had taken everything that was hers, but her hope of receiving military assistance from either of the Queens was small. Indeed, Elizabeth and Catherine were more interested in bidding against each other for Mary's fabulous black pearls. In the end Elizabeth offered more and obtained them from Moray.

Mary was not, however, relying entirely on foreign aid. On 25 March

158. *George, Lord Seton, with his family*, by Frans Pourbus, painted in 1572. (National Gallery of Scotland, on loan to the Scottish National Portrait Gallery)

she tried to escape from Lochleven by disguising herself as one of the washerwomen who came over to the castle from the shore. Her beautiful white hands gave her away, but the boatman who noticed them did not betray her, he merely returned her to her prison.

Nothing daunted, she was determined to try again and by now she had a group of useful allies anxious to help her. Sir William Douglas's brother, George, had fallen in love with her, Willie Douglas, his young orphaned cousin, was equally devoted and of course Lord Seton and the Hamiltons had pledged themselves to win her freedom. Even the devious Maitland of Lethington seemed to be on her side again, for he sent her a jewel representing Aesop's fable of the mouse which gnawed at the ropes binding the captive lion.

Their opportunity came when Lady Douglas, Mary's constant companion, gave birth to a child and was temporarily out of action. On 2

May, Willie Douglas arranged an elaborate May Day celebration which took place with such boisterous fun that by dinner-time the Queen pronounced herself exhausted and retired to her chamber. As she lay on her bed, excitedly waiting for the next part of the plan, she could hear the women in the next room gossiping about how a large group of horsemen had been seen in the village of Lochleven that morning. They said they were passing through on legal business, but someone had recognised Lord Seton riding at their head.

After a short rest, the Queen joined Sir William Douglas downstairs. Glancing out of the window, he noticed Willie Douglas lurking about among the boats tied up on the shore. He uttered a wrathful exclamation and Mary, knowing that Willie was actually chaining the vessels so that they could not pursue her, realised that she must create a diversion. She pretended to feel faint, and as Sir William was the only person in the room with her he was forced to go and fetch her a cup of wine. By the time he returned, Willie had vanished. For the rest of the afternoon, Sir William kept looking suspiciously from his window, but he saw nothing.

Shortly after that, a servant brought the Queen one of her own pearl earrings, telling her that it had been found in the Castle. Mary knew that this was George Douglas's signal that everything was ready. She went downstairs and disguised herself in an old red kirtle belonging to one of her women, then she concealed it beneath her own cloak. Telling her companions she needed fresh air, she went out to walk in the gardens with old Lady Douglas. Another alarm followed, for Lady Douglas espied some riders on the far shore. However, Mary quickly launched into a long complaint about how badly the Earl of Moray was treating her, and his fond mother sprang to his defence, all thought of the mysterious riders quite forgotten.

After that, they went in to supper. The meal was always served to the Queen first, with Sir William waiting upon her. Once he had retreated to his own chambers, she hurried upstairs to change her good cloak for an old, shabby one. Over in the other part of the Castle, Willie Douglas was serving Sir William with his supper. As he handed him his evening drink, he dropped his kerchief on the table, apparently by accident. It fell on top of Sir William's keys, and when Willie retrieved the kerchief he picked up the keys as well. No one noticed.

He walked calmly from the room, went out into the courtyard, and waved to one of the Queen's women who was watching from her apartments. The Queen came downstairs, followed by her woman, and she crossed the courtyard in full view of some servants. Willie produced Sir William's keys, unlocked the Castle gates and out they went. He locked the gates behind them and threw the keys into the mouth of a cannon which was standing nearby.

For a moment or two the Queen, her attendant and Willie stood close to the Castle wall, terrified that they had been observed. Everything was quiet. There were no shouts of alarm. Casually they strolled down to the boats. The Queen climbed into one of them and lay down on the floor under a seat so that she would not be seen. A few washerwomen were standing near the other boats and to her horror Mary realised that they had recognised her. Willie hissed at them to keep silent, and a moment later the boatman was rowing the Queen swiftly across the loch.

George Douglas and a friend were waiting on the other side with horses taken from Sir William's own stable. There was a hasty exchange of greetings, then they rode rapidly south to a rendezvous with Lord Seton. He escorted them to his castle of Niddry, near Winchburgh. George and Willie Douglas went with her. George would serve her for many years; Willie would stay with her till her death. It was nearly midnight when they got to Niddry, but already people had heard rumours and they came out of their houses to stand at the roadside and cheer as she went by. She was free at last.

After a brief stay at Niddry, she rode west to Hamilton and there she and Archbishop Hamilton composed a proclamation triumphantly asserting her position as Scotland's true monarch: 'Mary, by the grace of God, undoubted and righteous hereditary Queen of Scotland, succeeding thereto of the immoveable just line, being lawfully elected, crowned, invested and inaugurate thereto.' After condemning in the bitterest terms the 'ungrateful, unthankful and detestable tyrants and treasonable traitors' who had imprisoned her, she revoked her abdication and emphasised that the Hamiltons were heirs to her throne after her son.

In the end, this proclamation was never published. Possibly upon reflection the Queen felt it to be too vehement in tone, but she may also have decided that it favoured the Hamiltons too much. While it suited her purpose to encourage them in the thought that she might be persuaded to marry Lord John Hamilton, the Duke of Châtelherault's son, she did not wish to commit herself too deeply to them.

In any event, the proclamation was scarcely necessary now, for her supporters were flocking to her side and on 8 May nine earls, nine bishops, eighteen lords and many others signed a document swearing loyalty to her and promising to aid her cause. Seeing this gathering support, the Queen was all for taking the field against the rebels. According to one account, when she consulted her advisers about the situation they told her that there were only two ways by which she could regain effective power. It could be done by parliament, or by battle.

'By battle let us try it!' exclaimed the Queen.

She had high hopes of success, for her enemies had been taken by surprise at her escape. Moray had been in Glasgow when he heard the news and he was 'sore amazed'. Sir William Douglas was so appalled at the disappearance of his state prisoner that he drew his dagger and tried to stab himself. After the initial shock, however, they were gathering their own army and when Mary offered to negotiate a settlement they refused. As far as Moray was concerned, he was Regent of Scotland and no one was going to displace him. Mary therefore decided to march towards Dumbarton, hoping to draw him into a fight before he could gather reinforcements.

This plan did not succeed, and it was not until 13 May that the two armies confronted one another at the village of Langside, on the outskirts of Glasgow. Moray had fewer men, but what they lacked in numbers they made up for in experience and among his commanders were Morton and the invaluable Kirkcaldy of Grange. The Queen was not so well supplied. Her general, the Earl of Argyll, was brother-in-law of the Earl of Moray and he had often been associated with him in the past. His enthusiasm for Mary's cause was not as wholehearted as she could have wished and when, at the very start of the battle, he either fainted or suffered an epileptic seizure, there were plenty of people ready to decide that his illness was more diplomatic than real. Whatever the cause, his indisposition left the royal army without a proper leader and when Kirkcaldy of Grange's pikemen advanced, Argyll's followers turned and fled.

The Queen was watching the action from a nearby hillside and when she saw how badly her forces were faring she mounted her horse and rode down to urge her soldiers on. Indeed, one of her retinue later told Catherine de Medici that she would have led her men personally in a new charge had she not found them quarrelling violently amongst themselves. Deaf to her eloquence, they were readier to exchange blows with each other than to attack the enemy.

All was lost. For the first time in her life, Mary's courage deserted her and she fled. Lord Herries was among the group of men riding with her, and he suggested that she seek sanctuary in his own lands in Dumfriesshire. They rode throughout that night without stopping and during the next few nights travelling after dark, they covered the rough, mountainous countryside of south-west Scotland.

A month later the Queen described her dreadful journey in a letter to her uncle the Cardinal.

'I have endured injuries, calumnies, imprisonment, famine, cold, heat, flight,' she said, 'not knowing whither, ninety-two miles across the country without stopping or alighting, and then I have had to sleep upon the ground and drink sour milk and eat oatmeal without bread and have been three nights like owls', with no female for companionship.

Eventually they arrived at the Maxwell stronghold of Terregles and there they held a council of war. Fierce arguments ensued as to what they should do next, but the Queen had made up her mind and nothing would persuade her to change it. She would seek the help of Queen Elizabeth. Throughout the months in Lochleven Elizabeth had done her best to save her and, whatever past differences lay between them, she would never stand by and see her sister Queen deposed by rebellious subjects. Mary had already sent her a diamond ring she had once received from her, as a sign that she needed help, and now she would ride to England and speak to Elizabeth in person.

Mary herself admitted later that when her companions heard her intentions they were appalled and they begged her not to go ahead with her plan. No English monarch was to be trusted, they warned. James I of Scotland had spent long years of captivity in the south and Mary's own father had not risked going to York to meet Henry VIII although that had once been planned. He had understood the dangers. Whatever Elizabeth might have said in the past, she would be unable to resist the temptation of seizing and imprisoning the Queen of Scots if she set foot in England.

Mary thought otherwise. In vain did Lord Herries and his friends

159. Dundrennan Abbey, where Mary spent her last night in Scotland. (Historic Buildings and Monuments, SDD)

beseech her to go to France instead.

'I commanded my best friends to permit me to have my own way,' Mary confessed afterwards, and she vowed that by the end of August she would be back in Scotland at the head of an army.

Her advisers were silenced. On her instructions, Lord Herries sent a letter to the Deputy Governor of Carlisle asking permission for her to cross into England and seek refuge there. Impatient as ever, the Queen did not wait for an answer. Once more she set about disguising herself as an ordinary woman. She had already cut off her long auburn hair to avoid being recognised and now she put on a plain chemise and some borrowed clothing. Her last night in Scotland was spent in the Abbey of Dundrennan, composing another letter to Elizabeth begging for assistance. Next day, Sunday, 16 March, at about three in the afternoon, she and her friends went down to the shores of the River Solway and embarked in a small fishing boat.

10
CAPTIVITY

IT TOOK the fishing boat four hours to cross the Solway, so that it was about seven o'clock in the evening when the Queen landed on the far shore. Her terror of the past few days had passed and, having taken the decision to go to Elizabeth, she was in a mood of such exhilaration that even when she stumbled and fell as she left the boat she was not dismayed. She and her companions instead chose to see this as a sign that she had come to take possession of England.

They had landed at the little port of Workington, and they spent that

160. Carlisle Castle, where Mary was held prisoner: Queen Mary's tower. (Royal Commission on the Historical Monuments of England)

night in Workington Hall, which was owned by a friend of Lord Herries. Next morning, the Deputy Governor of Carlisle arrived with a force of several hundred horsemen and announced that he had come to escort the Queen to Carlisle Castle.

Mary was alarmed. She wanted to go at once to London, but she accepted that arrangements had to be made for her journey and she resigned herself to waiting for a few days. She was, she wrote to the Earl of Cassillis, 'right well received and honourably accompanied and treated,' and she repeated to him her promise to be back in Scotland at the head of an army, French if not English, 'about the fifteenth day of August'.

Her mood of happy optimism was not echoed at the English Court. News of her arrival threw Elizabeth and her advisers into a turmoil of alarm and indecision. The last person they wanted in their country was the woman who not only claimed to be heir to the throne but had actually been proclaimed rightful Queen of England by the French. From the outset there was no possibility that Elizabeth would help her, nor could she be allowed to seek assistance in France. No one knew what should be done with her instead, for Elizabeth had to consider the reaction of the French and Spanish Kings. She decided to play for time, and she sent an emissary to see Mary. She chose for this delicate mission Sir Francis Knollys, a Puritan gentleman whose loyalty was beyond doubt.

If Sir Francis travelled north expecting to meet a raffish, disreputable foreigner, he was soon disabused of any such notion.

'This lady and Princess is a notable woman,' he reported to Cecil with ill-concealed surprise. 'She seemeth to regard no ceremonious honour beside the acknowledging of her estate regal. She showeth a disposition to speak much, to be bold, to be pleasant and to be very familiar. She showeth a great desire to be avenged of her enemies. She showeth a readiness to expose herself to all perils in hope of victory. She delighteth much to hear of hardiness and valiancy, commending by name all approved hardy men of her country, although they be her enemies, and she commendeth no cowardness even in her friends.'

He had soon observed that 'the thing that most she thirsteth after is victory'. She did not mind how it was achieved, whether 'by the sword of her friends or by the liberal promises and rewards of her purse or by division and quarrels raised among themselves', because, 'for victory's sake, pain and pleasure seemeth pleasant unto her, and in respect of victory, wealth and all things seemeth to her contemptuous and vile'. He had rightly recognised that to the Queen of Scots, honour and her own regal status mattered far more than anything else.

During his stay at Carlisle, Sir Francis found himself impressed, in spite of himself, with what he described as Mary's intelligence, eloquence, courage and practical good sense. Indeed, he formed such a high opinion of her perspicacity that he doubted whether Cecil and the others ought to go on deceiving her about their intentions since it might not be wise 'to dissemble with such a lady'.

Mary herself was waiting with increasing impatience for Elizabeth's response, and after a month in England she told her uncle that 'to crown all', I am little else than a prisoner'. She had her own household of about

161. Bolton Castle, where Mary was kept when she was moved from Carlisle. (Photograph, Michael Brooks)

thirty attendants including Mary Seton, who had been allowed to join her, but the signs of captivity were unmistakable whatever Sir Francis might say. There were gratings on her windows, her antechambers were guarded by soldiers and, when she was allowed to ride outside she was escorted by a hundred horsemen.

Part of her time was spent in writing frantic letters to her allies pleading for assistance, and she was much concerned with the sufferings of her faithful followers. Moray and his men 'demolish all the houses of my servants,' she told her uncle, 'and I cannot aid them; and hang their owners and I cannot compensate them, and yet they all remain faithful to me, abominating these cruel traitors. When I parted from my people in Scotland I promised to send them assistance at the end of August. For God's sake let them not be denied and deceived. . . . It is all one for myself, but let not my subjects be deceived and ruined, for I have a son, whom it would be a pity to leave in the hands of these traitors. . . .'

May became June and still no reply came from Elizabeth until, on the 8th, an emissary arrived. The English Queen could not possibly receive the Queen of Scots in London, he said, until Mary was cleared of all the accusations against her, and that could only be done at an enquiry which Elizabeth would set up.

Mary was horrified. Apart from her overwhelming disappointment, she was shocked at the implication that Elizabeth had any jurisdiction over her. She was a monarch, the English Queen's equal. In a passion of misery and rage she wept bitter tears and sent off more distraught letters to

162. The Queen Mary Casket in which, it was claimed, incriminating letters from Mary to Bothwell were found. (The Duke of Hamilton, at Lennoxlove)

Elizabeth, to Catherine de Medici, Charles IX of France, her uncle the Cardinal, the Duke of Anjou, to anyone indeed who might intervene on her behalf. Shortly afterwards, Elizabeth had her moved from Carlisle to Bolton Castle in Yorkshire, further away from the Scottish border.

In the end, Mary realised that Elizabeth was adamant, she persuaded herself that an enquiry would be no more than a formality, and eventually she consented to take part. She was told that Elizabeth's representatives would go to York and hear submissions from the Earl of Moray and herself. They would then decide the truth of the matter.

Mary's mood was now one of happy confidence. Sir Francis Knollys had already noticed how easily she had convinced everyone in the north of her innocence and, believing herself to be entirely in the right, she had no fears of the outcome; no fears, that is, until she was told that she would not be allowed to appear in person, and until she heard that the Earl of Moray was saying that he had irrefutable evidence of her guilt in the silver casket he was bringing with him from Scotland.

This mysterious casket had been taken from one of Bothwell's servants, Moray said. It had obviously belonged to the Queen, for it was decorated with the crowned letter F, for Francis II, and inside it were what he claimed were her personal papers: eight letters and a long poem. They were love letters, apparently written from Mary to Bothwell while Darnley was ill

163. *Thomas, Duke of Norfolk,* whom Mary hoped to marry: engraved from a portrait in a private collection. (Scottish National Portrait Gallery)

with smallpox in Glasgow and they seemed to prove that she had deliberately gone there to lure him to his death.

The Casket Letters, as they are called, have long since disappeared. The originals vanished in the 1580s and they have never been seen since, but it is generally accepted that they were false, produced by Moray and Morton in an unscrupulous attempt to prevent the Queen from returning to Scotland. The copies which survive are incomplete, contradictory and do not even seem to read as consecutive prose. They were possibly pieced together, partly from innocuous letters from Mary to a friend, partly from pleading messages to Bothwell from one of his cast off mistresses. Mary's handwriting, large, bold and in the usual italic style of the time, would have been easy to imitate. She herself was never allowed to see them.

Few of her contemporaries seemed to place much weight upon them as evidence. Although the Duke of Norfolk, head of the English commissioners, declared himself horrified if they were true, he was willing less than a week later to embark upon a scheme aimed at marrying him to Mary. A talk with Maitland of Lethington seems to have calmed all his suspicions. Most significant of all, of course, is the fact that Moray and Morton did not produce the letters until the conference at York. They

164. *George, 6th Earl of Shrewsbury*, Mary's jailor for many years, by an unknown artist. (The National Trust, at Hardwick Hall, Derbyshire: photograph, Hawkley Studios)

claimed to have had them since just after Carberry Hill, but it is incredible that if they did they made no attempt to use them against Mary when she was their prisoner at Lochleven.

In the end, they did not even convince Elizabeth and her commissioners. When the enquiry finally reported at the beginning of January 1569, it concluded that Mary had failed to prove that her subjects had rebelled against her unjustly, but Moray had also been unable to show that the Queen had been involved in Darnley's death. Moray then returned to Scotland. Mary remained a prisoner.

She did not realise it herself, but all her hopes of liberty were at an end. She was moved to the damp, depressing castle of Tutbury, a rambling, medieval building looking out over a noxious marsh, and she was given a new jailer in the person of George, Earl of Shrewsbury. He was kind enough to her in his way, but in these gloomy surroundings her life settled into a routine of deadly, stultifying monotony.

From time to time she was moved to other residences, and her treatment was sometimes harsh, sometimes lenient, according to the political and

165. *Bess of Hardwick*, the Earl of Shrewsbury's wife, who shared Mary's fondness for needlework, by an unknown artist. (The National Trust, at Hardwick Hall, Derbyshire: photograph, Hawkley Studios)

religious situation. She looked after her faithful retinue, and spent hours embroidering intricate emblems, often in the company of Shrewsbury's formidable wife, Bess of Hardwick. For a few years she had the diverting company of little Arabella Stewart, Lord Darnley's niece, whom she loved dearly. She kept pets, little birds and small dogs sent over from France. She read, she danced and she sat up late playing cards. She continued to take an interest in her appearance, questioning friends about the latest fashions, and she always made sure that wherever she went, her cloth of state, that symbol of royal power, was erected over her chair.

Above all else, she was desperate to keep in touch with the outside world. She was usually permitted visitors, and there were some marvellous occasions when she was allowed to go to Buxton to bathe in the medicinal waters. There, she met courtiers up from London for the sake of their health and not only did she strike up a friendship with Sir William Cecil but she even met and got to know her former suitor the Earl of Leicester. Those were rare eventualities, though, and for the most part she relied upon her correspondence as her only source of hope that some day

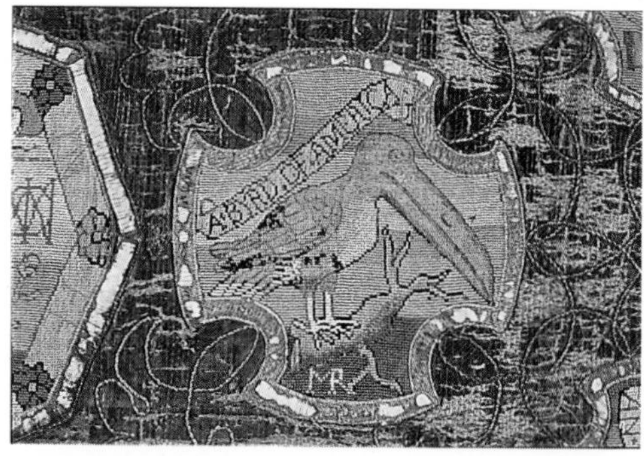

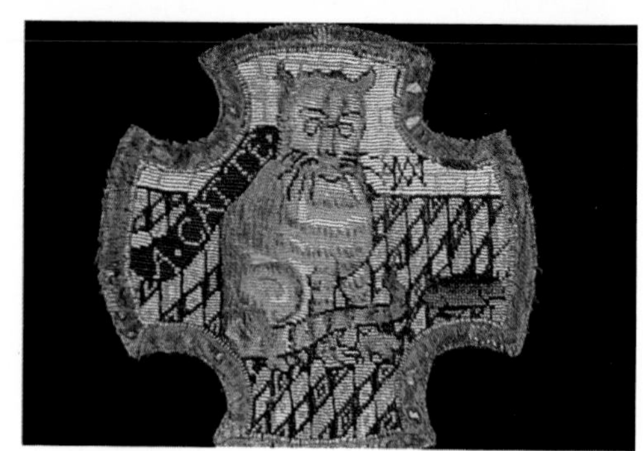

166. The Oxburgh Hangings, worked by Mary during her captivity:
(a) Mary's monogram
(b) 'a byrd of America'
(c) a cat
(d) a unicorn
(*(a)*, *(b)* and *(d)* by courtesy of the Board of Trustees of the Victoria and Albert Museum, *(c)* reproduced by gracious permission of Her Majesty The Queen)

her friends would come to her rescue and she would be set free.

During the early days of her imprisonment, she told Sir Francis Knollys, 'If I shall be holden here perforce, you may be sure then, being as a desperate person, I will use any attempts that may serve my purpose, either by myself or my friends' and she always regarded herself as being perfectly free to join in any plot to restore her.

In spite of the fact that she was still married to Bothwell, she welcomed the suggestion that she should marry Norfolk because she fondly imagined that Elizabeth would approve. The Bothwell marriage had not achieved its purpose and now he was gone from her life. If she had her marriage annulled and became Norfolk's wife, Elizabeth would surely see that she posed no threat. The Duke was a faithful supporter of Elizabeth and if he were Mary's consort they could rule Scotland together and enjoy the English Queen's friendship.

Mary had never actually met Norfolk, but she sent him encouraging messages and she embroidered a pillow for him with the arms of Scotland on it, telling him in her usual extravagant language,

'I trust none that shall say I ever mind to leave you. I vow never to do anything that may displease you, for I have determined never to offend you, but remain yours. . . .' That summer she sent messengers to Rome to

167. *Mary, Queen of Scots,* in 1578, a miniature by Nicholas Hilliard. (By courtesy of the Board of Trustees of the Victoria and Albert Museum)

seek an annulment of her marriage to Bothwell on the grounds that he had never been properly divorced from his first wife and that he had taken Mary by force.

Before any answer could come from the Pope, however, Queen Elizabeth found out what was afoot and, far from approving, she was furious. Any plotting behind her back was sure to provoke her wrath, but a marriage planned without her consent was well known to anger her beyond everything. Norfolk was imprisoned in the Tower of London, Mary's chambers were searched by armed men and her household was reduced in size. When the Roman Catholic Earls of Northumberland and Westmoreland offered to arrange her escape she refused. She could see that they were unlikely to succeed, and she dared not risk the consequences.

While Norfolk languished in the Tower she still regarded herself as being committed to him, and the beginning of 1571 brought her news from Scotland which she considered to be encouraging. The Regent Moray was assassinated, shot by a member of the Hamilton family as he rode through Linlithgow, on the orders of Archbishop Hamilton. All Mary's former affection for her half-brother had long since been swept away and instead of mourning his death she arranged to pay a pension to his murderer. With her principal enemy in Scotland gone, she nurtured hopes that her own restoration was more likely and before long she received further encouragement. The Pope not only excommunicated Queen Elizabeth but released her Catholic subjects from their allegiance to her.

168. Tutbury Castle, Mary's most hated prison. (Photograph, Michael Brooks)

This was an open invitation to Elizabeth's enemies to plot against her and soon a major new scheme was under way. Roberto Ridolfi, an Italian banker living in London, had the idea of using Spanish help to depose Elizabeth and place Mary on the throne instead. The Duke of Norfolk had recently been released from the Tower and before long he was involved. Letters flew back and forth but in the late spring Elizabeth was warned of what was happening, a messenger carrying letters from Ridolfi was seized, and all was revealed. Norfolk was arrested, sent back to the Tower, tried for treason and executed. The House of Commons urged Elizabeth to order the death of the Queen of Scots as well, but she refused. Instead, Mary was officially deprived of all her rights to the English throne and she was solemnly warned that if she were ever to involve herself in such a scheme again, she would not be tried by her equals, as was her right, but by a group of English noblemen.

To add to Mary's disappointment, the situation in Scotland was deteriorating again too. After a series of short-lived Regents, her old enemy the Earl of Morton took over the running of the country and Edinburgh Castle, the last fortress holding out for her, fell to the Protestants. After all his opposition to her, Kirkcaldy of Grange had changed sides and had been keeping it for her along with the changeable Maitland of Lethington. Now Kirkcaldy was executed and Maitland died before he could follow him to the scaffold. The Earl of Shrewsbury noted that when he broke the news of Maitland's death to Mary, 'she makes little show of any grief, and yet it nips her very near'.

169. *Lady Arabella Stewart,* Lord Darnley's niece, by an unknown artist, when she was twenty-three months old. (The National Trust, at Hardwick Hall, Derbyshire: photograph, R. A. Wilsher)

A new plan, instigated by the Pope, was aimed at marrying her to Philip II's dashing half-brother, Don John of Austria, but his death from typhoid ended that and it was perhaps just as well. Mary's position was becoming increasingly dangerous and any hint of further scheming on her part could prove fatal. The Catholic Church had recently launched a campaign to reconvert England, and in opposition to this the English parliament was tightening up its anti-Catholic laws. Elizabeth also gave the task of rooting out Catholic plotters to a new and dangerous agent, Sir Francis Walsingham. Clever, devious and utterly unscrupulous, he had built up a highly efficient spy network both at home and on the continent and his dearest ambition was to ensnare the Queen of Scots.

His principal method was to initiate false plots against Elizabeth in the hope that Mary would join in and become so deeply implicated that she could not escape. One of his agents was instrumental in setting up the Throckmorton Plot of 1583 and two years later there was an even more sinister development when he encouraged Dr Parry in a plan to murder

170. *Mary, Queen of Scots,* by an unknown artist: one of various pictures painted for her supporters during her life or, in this case, some years after her death. (Scottish National Portrait Gallery)

171. Buxton Baths, where Mary was sometimes allowed to bathe for the sake of her health. (Royal Commission on the Historical Monuments of England)

Elizabeth. Mary expressed her horror when this scheme came to light, but everyone believed that she was involved. The English parliament announced that in future she would be liable to execution for any plot on her behalf, whether she knew anything about it or not, and the conditions of her imprisonment became more severe. A new jailer was appointed, Sir Amyas Paulet, and Mary soon decided that this stern, unbending Puritan was 'one of the strangest and most *farouche* men' that she had ever known.

His first action was to tear down her precious cloth of state, although he was forced to return it when she protested. He told her that she would not be allowed to go outside, since by giving alms to the poor she 'hath won the hearts of the people that habit about those places where she hath heretofore lain'. He made petty regulations restricting the activities of her servants, he refused to believe that she was ill when she really did suffer constant poor health and, unlike any of his predecessors, he found her tiresome and irritating. Worst of all, he cut off her communication with the outside world. In future, she was to be allowed to send and receive messages only from the French ambassador in London, and from no one else, and he himself would open and read each letter that came to her from there. Throughout 1585 she did not receive one secret letter.

This forcible severing of her much prized connections with her friends affected her health and, by the end of that year, she had fallen so seriously ill that even Sir Amyas was forced to do something. She was moved to the more pleasant Chartley Hall, but even then she lay in bed for more than a month. Knowing her to be at a low ebb, Sir Francis Walsingham initiated the final stage in his plan to bring her down.

On 16 January 1586, a brewer arrived at the Hall bearing a packet for the Queen of Scots and to her incredulous delight she found that it contained a

172. *Mary, Queen of Scots, and her son James VI*, an imaginary portrait by an unknown artist, for she never saw her son after he was just under two years old.
(The Duke of Atholl, at Blair Castle: photograph, *Scotland's Story*)

173. South Wingfield, another of Mary's prisons. (Photograph, Michael Brooks)

174. *Sir Francis Walsingham*, who was determined to bring about Mary's downfall; portrait attributed to J. de Critz. (National Portrait Gallery, London)

secret letter from her friends. Better still, the brewer announced that he was willing to act as a courier for her, taking her reply and bringing in more letters. Joyfully she dictated her correspondence to Claud Nau, her French secretary. He put the private messages into code and gave them to the brewer, but instead of sending them straight to the French ambassador as Mary believed he would, he passed them at once to Walsingham's agent. He took them to Sir Amyas, who sent them on to Walsingham himself. There they were decoded, read, resealed and eventually dispatched to their original destination. From now on, every detail of Mary's intrigues would be known from the start.

Having settled the procedure, Walsingham turned his attention to concocting a new assassination plot. A group of young Catholic idealists resolved to rescue Mary and put her on the English throne. Their leader was Sir Anthony Babington, a former page with Lord Shrewsbury. To him, Mary was not only the unjustly imprisoned Queen of Scots but a Catholic martyr, persecuted first by the Protestants in her own country then by those in England. Walsingham's agents found out about Babington's plans and the spymaster's deliberately devised scheme was soon intermingled with Sir Anthony's.

By June, Mary was in correspondence with Babington, and he told her all about his plan, describing his hopes of a foreign invasion and speaking of the release of Mary. Implicit in everything he said was the understanding that Elizabeth would be removed from the scene. As soon as she received this letter, Mary's fate was sealed. Parliament had said that she would face execution if anyone started up a new plot to assassinate

175. *Sir Amyas Paulet,* Mary's last jailor, by an unknown artist from an earlier portrait. (Jersey Museum, La Société Jersiaise)

Elizabeth even if Mary was not personally involved. Nau, her secretary, advised her not to send a full reply but of course she was determined to use her own judgment. She might well have reached the conclusion that any possible chance of success was far outweighed by the dangers involved, but even as she pondered her hopes for the future received another shattering blow.

For some months past, her representatives had been trying to negotiate a settlement with Elizabeth and James VI whereby Mary could return to Scotland and rule jointly with her son. She had not seen him since he was a baby, but she had done her best to keep in constant touch with him. She cherished a deep affection for him and as the years went by she imagined him as the ideal child, a brave, handsome boy who would grow to manhood, devoted to her and come to her rescue as soon as he was able. She wrote him letters, made him presents and anxiously inquired about his welfare.

Instead of the happy, willing lad of her imagination, James was a silent, wary child, forced into ways of concealment and caution from his earliest days. Brought up as a Protestant by his mother's enemies, he had as his tutor George Buchanan, the man who had compiled a lengthy and highly coloured document accusing Mary of all manner of crimes in the most vituperative language possible. He taught James to hate and fear his mother so that, by the time he grew to manhood, far from working for her release he was determined that she should never return to challenge his right to rule the country he regarded as entirely his.

For a time, it suited him to go along with Mary's plans for restoration and a joint rule, but just as Sir Anthony Babington sent Mary his letter, she received devastating news. Her son had signed a treaty of alliance with Elizabeth and, far from including the provision that his mother should be released, the agreement made no mention of Mary whatsoever. To add insult to injury, James had accepted a pension from Elizabeth. As she told Archbishop Beaton, Mary was heartbroken. This betrayal by her own child was the worst treachery. A fortnight later she wrote back to Babington giving her approval to his plans.

Her reply, of course, was passed to Paulet then Walsingham. When Walsingham's agent decoded it, he saw at once that she had fallen into their trap and he drew a gallows on it. Walsingham was overjoyed and for good measure he forged a postscript in which Mary asked for details of the men who would kill Elizabeth. He then resealed the letter and sent it to Babington.

On 11 August, Sir Amyas Paulet unexpectedly invited his royal prisoner to go out deer hunting with him. She was surprised by his unusual cordiality, but she was pleased, too, and she dressed with care. When she was ready, she rode out accompanied by her two secretaries and her personal physician. The sun was shining, the day was hot, and when she noticed Paulet lagging behind she remembered that he had recently been ill and she sympathetically slowed her own pace. Before he could catch up, though, she suddenly saw a group of horsemen on the skyline, riding rapidly towards her. For one ecstatic moment she believed that Babington had arrived to rescue her, but her wild hopes were quickly dashed. Sir Thomas Gorges, emissary to Queen Elizabeth, was leader of the group. Resplendent in an embroidered suit of green, he came up to her with a portentous air, dismounted, then said in loud tones,

'Madame, the Queen my mistress finds it very strange that you, contrary to the pact and engagement made between you, should have conspired against her and her state, a thing which she could not have believed, had she not seen proofs of it with her own eyes and known it for certain.'

As Mary stared at him in horror, Gorges went on to say that her servants shared her guilt, whereupon the two secretaries were dragged away. Gorges said that Mary and her physician would be taken to a house at Tixall, some miles off. Believing that she was to be executed there and then, the Queen tried to resist, and she sat down on the grass and refused to move. Paulet then came to stand over her threateningly, all his former geniality gone. If she did not get up, he said, she would be removed by force. At that, she threw herself despairingly on her knees and began to pray. When her doctor tried to console her, she told him bitterly that she was no longer of use to anyone on earth.

For the next two weeks she was kept at Tixall, then she was taken back to Chartley. As her little cavalcade approached the familiar gatehouse once more, a crowd of poor men and women ran out on to the road to greet her, for they had often received her charity in the past.

'Alas, good people!' she exclaimed, 'I have now nothing to give you, for I am as much a beggar as you are yourselves!'

Once inside, she discovered that her little household was in disarray. Her belongings had been searched and, although her money was untouched, her other valuables had been confiscated, including her miniatures of Francis II and the French royal family. However, she told Paulet proudly that she still possessed the two things which he could never take away from her, her royal blood and her Roman Catholic religion.

During her absence, Barbara Curle, her secretary's wife, had given birth to a daughter but Sir Amyas had refused to allow the baby to be christened by a priest. When she heard, the Queen announced that she would baptise the child herself and that she did, giving her the name Mary. That small excitement over, she and her household waited anxiously to see what would happen next.

News from London filtered slowly through. Babington and his friends were tried, condemned and executed. The secretaries Nau and Curle were interrogated and they confessed. They were then thrown into prison. On 21 September Sir Thomas Gorges arrived back at Chartley again. Mary's servants were locked in their rooms and Paulet announced that she was being moved elsewhere. Her destination was not revealed to her, but after four days' travelling she arrived at the formidable castle of Fotheringhay in Northamptonshire. She knew that it was used only as a state prison, and when they told her that the road leading to it was called Perryho Lane, she exclaimed, 'Perio! I perish!'

Strangely, her mood was more cheerful than it had been for many

176. The gatehouse at Tixall, where Mary was taken in 1586. (Photograph, Michael Brooks)

months. At last, she saw an end to the wretched years of captivity.

'Alas, what am I? What's my life become?' she had written shortly before in one of her French poems,

'A corpse, existing where the pulse hath fled,
An empty shadow, mask for conflicts dread,
Whose only hope of refuge is the tomb!'

and death was now a welcome prospect. Moreover, she was determined that she would die in triumph, not as a common criminal but as the person of pre-eminence she had always been. She believed unflinchingly that she was innocent of all the charges against her, and that no one had any right to try her. She would go to her death as a Catholic martyr, she resolved, the victim of Protestant lies and treachery, and then the whole world would know that she was still a mighty Princess, persecuted but undefeated. When Sir Amyas Paulet told her that the date of her trial had been fixed, she replied proudly,

177. The mound upon which Fotheringhay Castle stood: James VI had the castle demolished. (Photograph, Michael Brooks)

178. *Queeen Elizabeth* in about 1588, by or from a painting by G. Gower. (National Portrait Gallery, London)

'As a sinner I am truly conscious of having offended my Creator, and I beg Him to forgive me, but as Queen and Sovereign I am aware of no fault or offence for which I have to render account to anyone below. . . . As therefore I could not offend, I do not wish for pardon. I do not seek it, nor would I accept it from anyone living.'

When a trial had first been mentioned she had refused to appear, explaining,

'I am myself a Queen, the daughter of a King, a stranger and the true

179. Miniature of Mary, painted towards the end of her life.
(The Trustees of Blairs College, Aberdeen: photograph, *Scotland's Story*)

kinswoman of the Queen of England. I came to England on my cousin's promise of assistance against my enemies and rebel subjects and was at once imprisoned. . . . As an absolute Queen I cannot submit to orders, nor can I submit to the laws of the land without injury to myself, the King my son and all other Sovereign Princes.' When she learned, however, that she would be condemned in her absence, she submitted.

On 15 October 1586 the Great Hall at Fotheringhay was filled with peers, privy councillors, clerks and court officials. At nine o'clock in the morning, the Queen of Scots entered, clad in her customary black, her long train carried by one of her women. She was supported by her physician and her steward, for rheumatism had made her very lame now. Her tall figure was heavier, too, the alluring beauty of her youth transformed into a more statuesque grandeur.

At the far end of the hall stood a throne, with a cloth of state above it, bearing the arms of England.

'I am a Queen by right of birth and my place should be there!' she exclaimed, but she was shown across to a red velvet chair instead and since Elizabeth was absent the throne remained empty. She sat down and began to scan the faces of the men opposite, many of them well-known to her by name although she had never met them, and throughout the proceedings she was to ask her companions the identity of this one and that.

From the beginning she was at a disadvantage, for she was allowed neither lawyers, secretaries nor defence witnesses nor was she permitted to consult any of her papers. For the next two days she argued her case without them, insisting over and over again that she had never planned Elizabeth's death.

'I do not deny that I have earnestly wished for liberty,' she said, when questioned, 'and done my utmost to procure it for myself. In this I have acted from a very natural wish, but,' she added, 'can I be responsible for the criminal projects of a few desperate men, which they planned without my knowledge or participation?'

Nothing the English commissioners said could shake her calm but by the end of that first afternoon they were all shouting agitatedly at her in a storm of accusations and she looked visibly shaken when she retired to her apartments.

The next morning, she addressed the court herself, insisting once more that they had no right to try her because she was a monarch, and telling them many times that she was innocent of any assassination plot. After making a final request for a hearing before Elizabeth, she rose to her feet and with great dignity told her accusers that she forgave them for what they had done. Shen then crossed over to where Walsingham sat and said a few words to him, before turning again to the assembled company. In a quiet voice she asked God to pardon them for treating her 'somewhat rudely,' and then with a small, ironic smile, she added, 'May God keep me from having to do with you again.' With that, she walked slowly from the hall.

The courtiers rode back to London and on 25 October they reassembled in the Star Chamber at Westminster to announce their verdict. The Queen of Scots was guilty of plotting the assassination of Elizabeth, they said. Both houses of parliament then presented an address to the English Queen, begging her to order Mary's execution.

While Mary waited calmly at Fotheringhay, sewing, reading English history, arguing with Paulet and attempting to cheer her own household,

180. The last letter of Mary, Queen of Scots, written to her brother-in-law Charles IX, at 2 am on the morning of her execution. (National Library of Scotland)

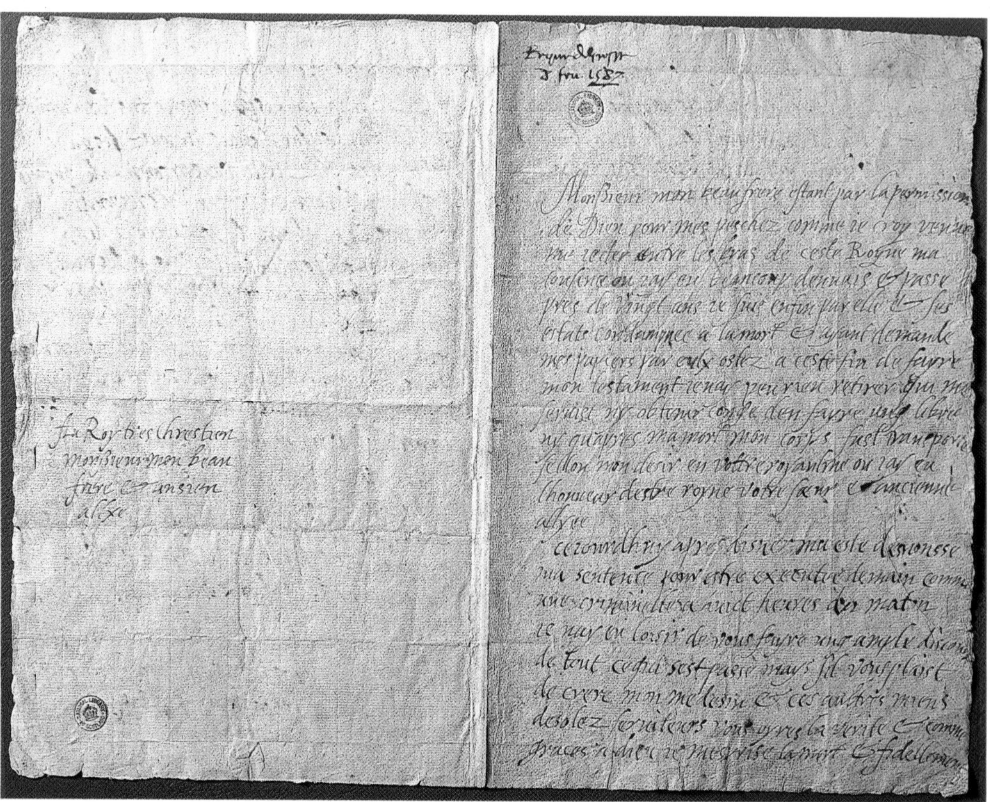

Au Roy tres chrestien monsieur mon beau frere et ancien allye

Monsieur mon beau frere estant par la permission de Dieu pour mes pechez comme je croy venue me getter entre les bras de ceste Royne ma cousine ou j'ay eu beaucoup d'ennuys et passe pres de vingt ans je suis enfin par elle et ses estats condamnee a la mort et ayant demande mes papiers par eulx ostez a ceste fin de feyre mon testament je nay peu rien retirer qui me servist ny obtenir conge den fayre ung libre ny quapres ma mort mon corps fust transporte selon mon desir en votre royaulme ou j'ay eu l'honneur destre royne votre soeur et ancienne allyee

ceiourdhuy apres disner ma este denoncee ma sentence pour estre executee demain comme une criminelle a huict heures du matin je nay eu loisir de vous fayre ung ample discours de tout ce qui sest passe mays sil vous plaist de croire mon medesin et ces aultres miens desolez serviteurs vous oyres la verite et comme graces a dieu je mesprise la mort et fidellement

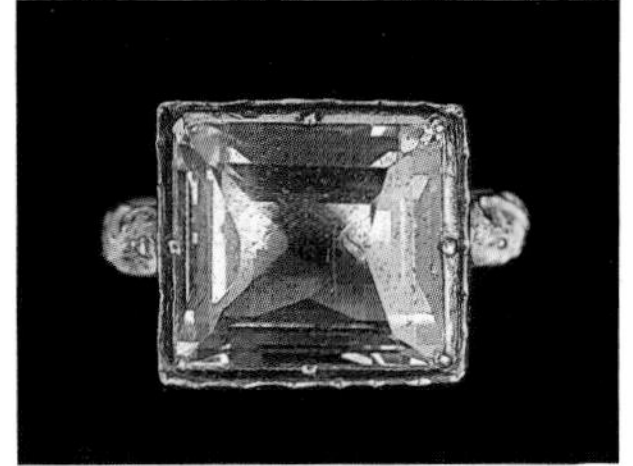

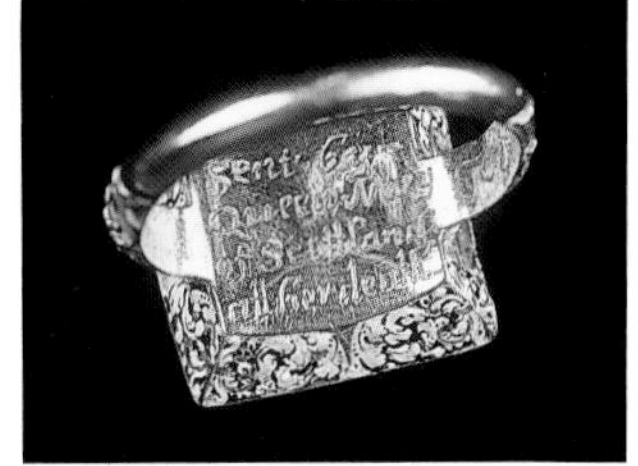

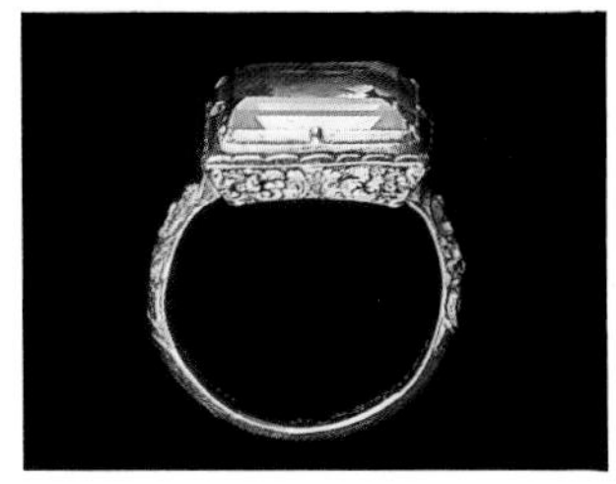

181. Sapphire ring with inscription relating that it was sent by Mary to Lord John Hamilton on the eve of her execution. (The Duke of Hamilton, at Lennoxlove)

Elizabeth tried to nerve herself to sign her cousin's death warrant. It was not sentiment which made her hesitate, for she believed that Mary really had aimed at her death. She delayed because by executing a fellow monarch she would create a dangerous precedent, and she was nervous of the reaction from abroad. Plagued by the conflict between her desire to eliminate a dangerous enemy and her fear of the consequences if she did, Elizabeth wept, argued and put off taking a decision until in the end her well-developed sense of self-preservation won the day.

On 1 February 1587 her secretary handed her a pile of papers. She went through them, signing each one with scarcely a glance, pretending that she did not know that the fateful document was among them. Afterwards she would claim that she had signed it by mistake, but in reality she knew exactly what she was doing and even at this late date she wrote to Paulet

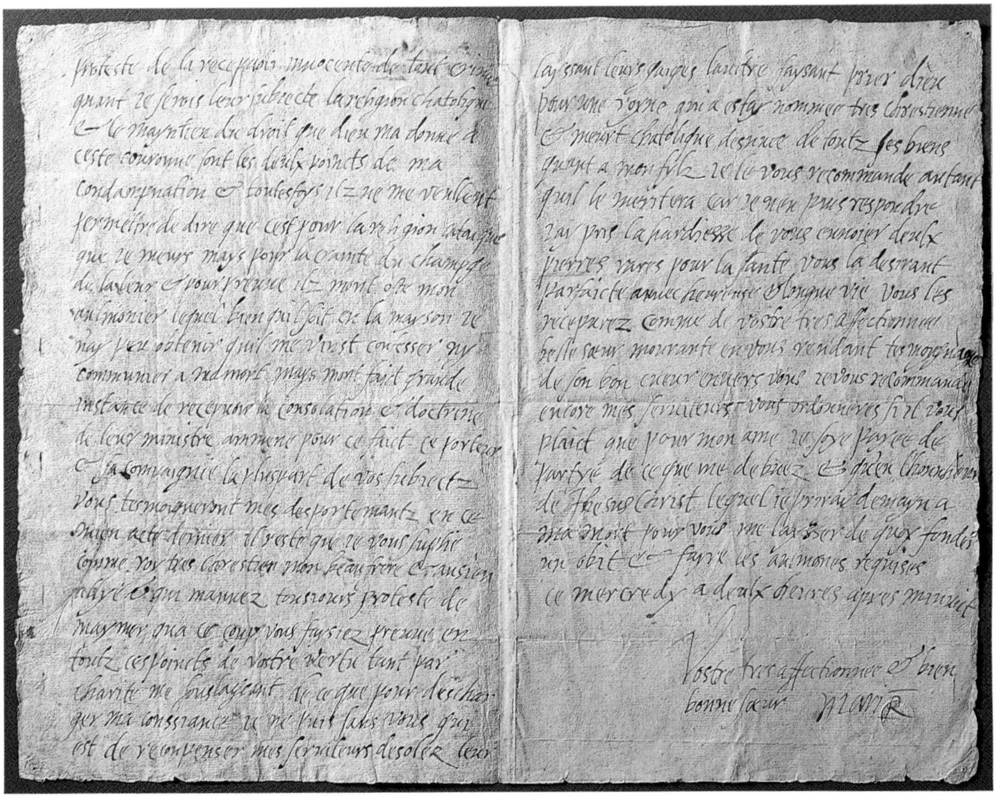

protester de la receue innocente de tout crime quant je serois leur subiecte la religion catholique et le maintien du droit que dieu ma donne a ceste couronne sont les deulx poincts de ma condampnation et toutesfoys ilz ne me veulent permettre de dire que cest pour la religion catholique que je meurs mays pour la crainte du change de la leur et pour preuve ilz mont oste mon aulmonier lequel bien quil soit en la mayson je nay peu obtenir quil me vinst confesser ny communier a ma mort mays mont faict grande instance de recevoir la consolation et doctrine de leur ministre amene pour ce faict. ce porteur et sa compaignie la plus part de vos subiectz vous tesmoigneront mes deportemantz en ce mien acte dernier. il reste que je vous suplie comme roy tres chrestien mon beau frere et ansien allye et qui mavez tousiours proteste de maymer qua ce coup vous faysiez preuve en toutz ces poincts de vostre vertu tant par charite me soulageant de ce que pour descharger ma consiance je ne puis sans vous qui est de recompenser mes serviteurs desolez leur

laysant leurs gaiges laultre faysant prier dieu pour une royne qui a estay nommee tres chrestienne et meurt catholique desnuee de toutz ses biens. quant a mon filz je le vous recommande autant quil le meritera car je nen puis respondre. jay pris la hardiesse de vous envoier deulx pierres rares pour la sante vous la desirant parfaicte avec heureuse et longue vie. vous les recepvrez comme de vostre tres affectionnee belle soeur mourante en vous rendant tesmoignage de son bon cueur envers vous. je vous recommande encore mes serviteurs vous ordonnerez sil vous plaict que pour mon ame je soye payee de partye de ce que me debvez et quen lhonneur de Jhesus Christ lequel je priray demain a ma mort pour vous me laysser de quoy fonder un obit et fayre les aulmosnes requises. ce mercredy a deulx heures apres minuit.

Vostre tres affectionnee et bien bonne soeur MarieR

182. The Penicuik Jewels, sixteenth-century jewellery said to have been given by Mary to her serving woman Giles Mowbray just before her execution. (National Museums of Scotland)

telling him of her disappointment that he had found no private means of shortening Mary's life. Much as he disliked the Queen of Scots, Sir Amyas was outraged.

'God forbid that I should make so foul a shipwreck of my conscience!' he replied, whereupon Elizabeth cursed what she called his 'daintiness'. During that week, a loud hammering was heard throughout Fotheringhay Castle as the carpenters built the scaffold. The Earl of Shrewsbury and other courtiers were arriving from London and on 7 February, after dinner, he, Paulet and two of their companions went to the Queen and read out her death warrant.

'I thank you for such welcome news,' she replied. 'You will do me great good in withdrawing me from this world out of which I am very glad to

183. Rosary and prayer book: Mary wore the gold rosary at her execution. The prayer book is reputed to have been given to her by Lord Herries during her flight to England. (Reproduced by permission of His Grace the Duke of Norfolk and the Baroness Herries)

go', and she put her hand on a copy of the New Testament and swore that she was innocent of any crime. When she asked them when she was to die, no one had the courage to tell her until, at last, Shrewsbury in a broken voice murmured that the execution would take place the following morning.

She spent her last night with her faithful servants. She ate a little supper, arranged her belongings, composed an elaborate testament and then wrote to her chaplain, whose services she had been denied. At two in the morning, she finished her last letter, to the King of France, telling him, 'I scorn death and vow that I meet it innocent of any crime.' After that she lay down on her bed, fully clothed, and listened to one of her ladies read from the Bible.

A six o'clock she rose, gave her final gifts to her weeping attendants and went to pray in her oratory. She was still there when the summons came between eight and nine o'clock. Her groom took down the large crucifix which hung above her altar and holding it aloft he led her small procession from the room. The Queen was wearing a long black dress over a red petticoat. A transparent veil floated from her shoulders to the hem of her skirt and on her head was a white cap. Beneath her gown, unseen by her guards, trotted one of her little pet dogs.

When she reached the doorway to the Great Hall her servants were told that they could not go in. They pleaded tearfully to be allowed to stay with

184. *The Execution of Mary, Queen of Scots*, by an unknown artist. (Scottish National Portrait Gallery)

185. Funeral sermon preached for Mary at Notre Dame, Paris, by the Archbishop of Bourges. (National Library of Scotland)

186. Title page of one of the many accounts of Mary's death published on the continent: this one is in Italian, printed in 1587. (National Library of Scotland)

ORAISON
FVNEBRE,
DE LA TRES-CHRE-
STIENNE, TRES-ILLVSTRE,
tres-constante, Marie Royne d'Escosse,
morte pour la Foy, le 18. Feburier, 1587.
par la cruauté des Anglois heretiques,
ennemys de Dieu.

Sur le subiect & discours de celle mesme qui fut faicte en Mars, à Nostre Dame de Paris, au iour de ses obseques & seruice, & lors prononcee par R. P. Messire Renauld de Beaulne, Archeuesque de Bourges, Patriarche d'Aquitaine, Conseiller du Roy en son Conseil Priué, & d'Estat.

A PARIS,
Chez Guillaume Bichon, ruë S. Iacques,
à l'enseigne du Bichot.

M. D. LXXXVIII.

VERA, E COMPITA
RELATIONE
Del successo della Morte della Christianissima Regina di Scotia.

Con la dichiaratione delle Essequie fatte in Parigi, dal Christianissimo Rè suo Cognato, & il nome de Personagi interuenuti.

Con licenza de Superiori.

In Milano, Per Giacomo Picaglia.
1587.

187. Memorial painting of Mary, by an unknown artist, commissioned by her lady-in-waiting, Elizabeth Curle, who was with her at her execution. (The Trustees of Blairs College, Aberdeen)

her and, when she promised that they would make no disturbance, adding, 'Alas, poor souls, it would do them good to bid me farewell,' the Earl of Kent gave way. She was allowed to choose six, and she selected her physician, her steward, two men servants and her two favourite women.

Silently, the little procession entered the Great Hall, where about three hundred people waited. The Queen mounted the scaffold and the Dean of Peterborough stepped forward but she waved him away.

'I am settled in the ancient Catholic Roman religion and mind to spend

188. Monument in St Andrew's Church, Antwerp, to Elizabeth and Barbara Curle, Mary's attendants, with her portrait at the top. (Institut Royal du Patrimonie Artistique, Brussels)

189. Engraving of the monument to Mary erected in Westminster Abbey by her son, James VI. (National Library of Scotland)

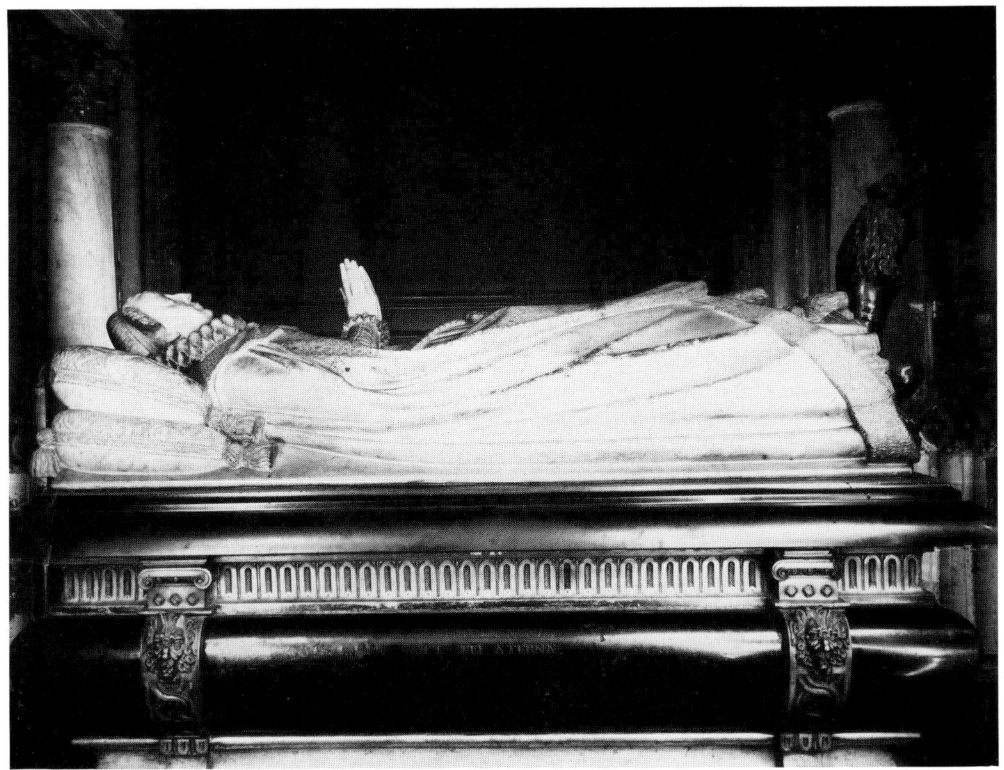

190. Effigy of Mary on the Westminster Monument. (By courtesy of the Dean and Chapter of Westminster)

my blood in defence of it,' she told him, and when he began to pray in English she knelt down and prayed loudly first in Latin then in English.

After she had finished, the executioner came across and asked her to pardon what he was about to do.

'I forgive you with all my heart,' she replied, 'for now I hope you shall make an end of all my troubles.'

As he and his assistant helped her women to remove her dress, her cap and her veil she smiled, commenting wryly that she had never before employed such grooms of the chamber. This made her ladies weep more than ever, so she murmured,

'Do not cry any more for me,' and reminded them, 'I have promised for you.' They should rejoice, she said, for her troubles would soon be over.

One of them bound a gold-embroidered cloth round her eyes and the Queen knelt down and placed her head upon the block.

'Into your hands, O Lord, do I commend my soul!' she cried loudly, several times over, and the executioner raised his axe. With the second stroke she was dead.

FURTHER READING

Mary, Queen of Scots and several of her friends and enemies have left us their descriptions of the dramatic events in which they were involved. Each was writing from a very personal point of view, sometimes many years later, but as long as we remember that they were not attempting to be impartial, we can find all manner of fascinating detail in their recollections.

The Queen dictated her reminiscences to her secretary, Claud Nau, towards the end of her life when she was in captivity in England. They are incomplete, but they give her version of the period from the aftermath of Riccio's murder to her flight into England. Nau's *Memorials of Mary Stewart* were edited by J Stevenson and published in Edinburgh in 1883. Further descriptions by Mary are to be found in her correspondence, which is printed in Prince Labanoff's *Lettres et Memoires de Marie, Reine d'Ecosse* (seven volumes, 1844). Lord Ruthven tried to justify his part in Riccio's murder in his *Relation,* written after his flight to England during the last few weeks of his life and published in R Keith's *History of the Affairs of Church and State in Scotland down to 1567,* edited by J P Lawson in 1844, while a brief piece by Bothwell, produced during his Danish imprisonment, appears in James Hepburn, Earl of Bothwell, *Les Affaires du Conte de Boduel,* edited by H Cockburn and T Maitland for the Bannatyne Club, Edinburgh 1829.

John Knox included in his *History of the Reformation in Scotland,* translated and edited by W Croft Dickinson, Edinburgh 1949, his vivid recollections of his debates with Mary. Sympathetic to her was Sir James Melville of Halhill, who also took a more lenient view than most of Lord Darnley in his *Memoirs,* edited by Gordon Donaldson, 1969. Details of the Queen's last months appear in the journal of her doctor, Bourgoing, published in M R Chantelauze, *Marie Stuart, son procès et son Exécution.* Finally, Mary's friends Lord Herries and Bishop Leslie wrote histories of what had happened: John Maxwell, Baron Herries, *Historical Memoirs of the Reign of Mary, Queen of Scots* (Abbotsford Club, 1836) and John Leslie, Bishop of Ross, *The Historie of Scotland* (Scottish Text Society, 1895).

Apart from these autobiographical works, the various printed *Calendars of State Papers* contain the letters and reports of English and foreign observers, while R Pitcairn's *Ancient Trials in Scotland* (Edinburgh 1833) has the depositions of various minor men involved at Kirk o'Field.

Hundreds of books have been written about the life of Queen Mary, and an extensive list is to be found in Antonia Fraser's long and excellent *Mary, Queen of Scots* (1969) which, along with Gordon Donaldson's classic works, *The First Trial of Mary, Queen of Scots* (1969), *Mary, Queen of Scots* (1974) and *All the Queen's Men* (1983, an analysis of her supporters) are the best modern assessments. Margaret Swain's *The Needlework of Mary, Queen of Scots* (first published in 1973) is a fascinating survey of the authentic embroideries produced by Mary, Ian B Cowan brings together differing views of the Queen in *The Enigma of Mary Stuart* (1971), and for those interested in her mother the only modern biography is the present writer's book, *Mary of Guise* (1977).

Finally, among the new books published for 1987 is an absorbing account of the buildings associated with Mary: D J Breeze and G Donaldson's *A Queen's Progress.*

Printed in the U.K by Lithoprint (Scotland) Ltd
287004/4591 C150 10/86.